- Want to become one of our authors or subject matter experts?

- Do you have a manuscript you'd like to see published?

- Have an idea for a product you want to pitch?

- **Send us a message. Your budding idea might be a new bestseller!**

We publish for all services:
Army, Air Force, Navy, and Marines
Email us: admin@mentorinc.us

Smoking the Board: Army Board Pocket Study Guide
Copyright © 2020–2021 by Mentor Enterprises, Inc.

Printed in USA by Mentor Enterprises Inc.

MENTOR
ENTERPRISES, INC.

123 Castle Dr. STE C, Madison, AL 35758
256.830.8282
admin@mentorinc.us

1st Edition, 1st Printing, 2021
ISBN-13: 978-1-940370-28-6

The views expressed in this book are those of the author
and do not reflect the official policy or position of the
United States Army, Defense Department, or the United
States Government.

Cover Photo by Timothy Hale US Army

SMOKING
THE BOARD

Army Board Pocket Study Guide

CSM (R) Mark Gerecht

Disclaimer

The content of this product is a compilation of information and personal experience from the author, numerous contributors and editors.

It is possible that mistakes may be found in both content and typography.

This book should and can only be used as a **guide**. Information gleaned from this product should be modified according to existing situations by seeking guidance from competent professionals including your chain of command, military lawyers, inspector generals, or other competent staff professionals.

No warranty is made or implied with regard to completeness and/or correctness, legal effect, or validity of this product in any state or jurisdiction. It is further understood that any person or entity that uses this product does so at their own risk with full knowledge that they have a legal obligation, duty, and responsibility to ensure the information they use or provide to others is in accordance with up-to-date military law, procedure, regulation, policy, and order. No part of this product shall in any way substitute for professional guidance or regulatory requirement.

Contents

Where can I find updates?

Updates and corrections to this book can be found at:
www.AskTOP.net/smoking-1ed/

When prompted use the following passcode:

PX98FW49

Army Body Composition Program

AR 600-9

What regulation covers the Army Body Composition Program?

AR 600-9.

What does the acronym ABCP mean?

Army Body Composition Program.

How often will Soldiers be screened to ensure compliance with AR 600-9?

At a minimum, Soldiers will be screened every six months.

What action will a commander take if a Soldier exceeds the body fat standard in accordance with AR 600-9?

The commander will flag the Soldier in accordance with AR 600-8-2.

What tool do commanders use to screen Soldiers for their semi-annual body fat assessment?

The authorized screening table for their age and measured height.

When is a Soldier released from the ABCP?

When they meet the body fat standard of AR 600-9.

When enrolled in the ABCP, how long does the Soldier have to read TG 358?

14 days.

How long does a Soldier have to complete the Soldier action plan?

It must be accomplished within 14 days of the notification counseling.

How often will ABCP assessments be conducted?

Approximately every 30 days.

Define satisfactory progress in the ABCP?

The monthly loss of three to eight pounds or one percent body fat. When more than one number, use the number.

How is failure in the ABCP defined?

If a Soldier exhibits less than satisfactory progress on two consecutive monthly assessments, or after six months in the ABCP and they still exceed body fat standards and have exhibited less than satisfactory progress for three or more nonconsecutive monthly assessments.

How are circumference measurements taken?

All circumference measurements will be taken sequentially three times and recorded to the nearest half-inch.

Circumference measurements are taken to the nearest ___inch?

Half inch.

A Soldier's height is measured to the nearest _____ inch?

Half inch.

How many days can be allowed between an APFT and a weigh-in?

Commanders are encouraged to allow a minimum of seven days between an APFT and the weigh-in.

Who will measure a Soldier?

A trained person of the same gender.

How long after enrollment in the ABCP does a Soldier have to meet with a dietitian?

It must be completed within 30 days of enrollment in the ABCP.

What action can be taken if a Soldier has a temporary medical condition that causes weight gain or prevents weight or body fat loss that will take longer than 6 months to resolve?

The initial 6-month period can be extended by a physician for up to 12 months.

What action will a commander take if a Soldier in ABCP is a program failure with no underlying medical condition?

The commander will initiate separation action, bar to reenlistment, or involuntary transfer to the IRR.

What action will be taken against a Soldier with no underlying medical condition, who exceeds the body fat standard within 12 months of release from the ABCP?

The Soldier will be processed for separation, barred from reenlistment, or transferred to the IRR.

What action will be taken against a Soldier with no underlying medical condition, who exceeds the body fat standard after 12 months but less than 36 months from the date of release from the ABCP?

The commander will initiate a flag, re-enroll the Soldier in the ABCP and the Soldier will have 90 days to meet the standard.

What action is taken when a Soldier in the ABCP desires to reenlist or extend?

No Soldier in the ABCP will be allowed to reenlist or extend. Note in rare cases the General Courts Martial Convening Authority or 1st General Officer in the chain of command can make an exception to policy.

How many people are required to take circumference measurements? Explain their duties

Two trained individuals; one to place the tape measure and determine measurements and the other to assure proper placement and tension of the tape.

What action is taken if during the taping process any one of the three measurements differs by more than one inch?

An additional measurement will be taken, compute a mathematical average of the three measurements with the least difference to the nearest half-inch and record this value.

In what uniform will tape measurements be taken?

Stocking feet in the standard Army physical fitness uniform trunks and t-shirt.

How often will scales be calibrated?

Annually.

When taking weight measurements for the body fat assessment the weight will be rounded to the nearest?

Pound.

What areas are measured during the body fat assessment on a male Soldier?

The neck and the abdomen.

What areas are measured during the body fat assessment on a female Soldier?

The neck, waist (abdomen), and hips.

How are consecutive measurements taken?

The Soldier measuring will take a complete set of all measurements and then begin the process again. This discourages the assumption of a repeated measurement.

How is the abdomen measured in relationship to the navel?

The measurement is taken at the navel level and parallel to the floor with arms at the side.

If a Soldier is enrolled in the ABCP and becomes pregnant, when will the Soldier be removed from the ABCP program?

When the Soldier meets body fat standards; Soldiers who become pregnant while in the ABCP program will not be removed from the program.

How are tape measures calibrated?

It will be compared with yardsticks or metal rulers to ensure validity.

Name two of four eating disorders.

Anorexia nervosa, bulimia nervosa, binge eating, and eating disorders not otherwise specified.

Army Programs

Army Continuing Education System (ACES)

....

TC 7-21.13, AR 621-5

What does the acronym ACES stand for?

Army Continuing Education System.

What services does ACES provide?

Programs and services to promote lifelong learning opportunities and to sharpen the competitive edge of the Army. Services include: Army Credentialing Opportunities On-line (COOL); tests of general education development; high school completion program; and functional academic skills training (FAST).

What regulation covers ACES?

AR 621-5.

Army Community Service (ACS)

....

TC 7-21.13, TC 7-22.7, AR 608-1

Explain the services provided by Army Community Service

Facilitates a commander's ability to provide comprehensive, coordinated, and responsive services that support the readiness of the Soldier. These services include: Mobilization and Deployment Readiness, Soldier Family Readiness, Relocation Readiness, Employment Readiness, Financial Readiness, Volunteer Programs, Soldier and Family Assistance Centers, and Survivor Outreach Services.

What does the acronym ACS stand for?

Army Community Services

What does the acronym SOS stand for with regard to ACS?

Survivor Outreach Services.

What regulation covers ACS?

AR 608-1.

Army Emergency Relief (AER)

TC 7-21.13, TC 7-22.7, AR 930-4

What does the acronym AER stand for?

Army Emergency Relief.

What services does AER provide?

The Army's own financial assistance organization and is dedicated to helping the Army take care of its own. Provides interest free loans, grants, or a combination of both to Soldiers who meet the qualification criteria.

Who may be eligible for AER assistance?

Soldiers on active duty and their eligible dependents; reserve component Soldiers (ARNG and USAR) on continuous AD orders for more than 30 consecutive days and their eligible dependents; Soldiers retired from AD because of longevity or retired at age 60 (Reserve Component) and their eligible family members; surviving spouses and surviving children of eligible Soldiers who died while on AD or after they were retired; Medically retired Soldiers and their eligible family members.

Who can approve loans or grants up to $4,000?

Garrison commander (or equivalent), deputy commander, garrison command sergeant major, or chief of staff.

Who can approve loans and grants up to $3,000?

AER officer or assistant AER officer may approve loans and grants up to $3,000.

Who can approve loans and grants over $4,000?

Loans and grants over $4,000 must be approved by HQ, AER.

If an individual is on the AER restricted list because they failed to repay a loan, who's approval is required if additional AER loan or grant is requested?

HQ, AER.

Army Family Action Plan (AFAP)

TC 7-21.13, TC 7-22.7, AR 608-1

What does the acronym AFAP stand for?

Army Family Action Plan.

What services does the Army Family Action Plan (AFAP) provide?

Provides active duty, reserve component Soldiers, Army civilians, Family members, survivors, and retirees a voice in shaping their standards of living by identifying issues and concerns for Army senior leadership resolution.

What is the Army Community Covenant?

A program designed to foster and sustain effective state and community partnerships with the Army to improve the quality of life for Soldiers and their families.

What regulation covers AFAP?

AR 608-1.

What agency oversees AFAP?

Army Community Service (ACS).

Army Family Team Building (AFTB)

....

TC 7-21.13, TC 7-22.7, AR 608-1, ATP 6-22.6

What does the acronym AFTB stand for?

Army Family Team Building.

What is the purpose of AFTB?

A family training and readiness program that provides participants with a better understanding of Army culture, as well as skills and resources needed to become resilient and self-reliant members of the military community.

What regulation covers AFTB?

AR 608-1, Appendix M.

What agency oversees AFTB?

Army Community Service (ACS).

How many levels are there in the AFTB program and name them?

There are three levels and they are Level 1, Level 2, and Level 3.

What ATP and TC's cover Army teambuilding?

ATP 6- 22.6, TC 7-21.13, TC 7-22.7.

What are the teambuilding stages?

Formation, enrichment, and sustainment.

What are the categories of teams?

Internal and external.

Army World Class Athlete Program (AWCAP)

....

TC 7-21.13

What does the acronym AWCAP stand for?

Army World Class Athlete Program.

What is the Army World Class Athlete Program?

Provides support and training to outstanding Soldier-athletes to help them compete and succeed in national and international competitions leading to Olympic and Paralympics Games.

Better Opportunities for Single Soldiers (BOSS)

....

TC 7-21.13, TC 7-22.7, AR 215-1

What does the acronym BOSS stand for?

Better Opportunities for Single Soldiers.

Explain the BOSS program.

A quality of life program that addresses single Soldier issues and initiatives.

Explain the Quality of Life program as it relates to the BOSS program.

Includes those issues that can influence directly or indirectly morale, living environment, or personal growth and development of Soldiers.

Explain the Recreation and Leisure program as it relates to the BOSS program.

Fun activities are planned by the BOSS council working in conjunction with Morale, Welfare, and Recreation.

What regulation covers the BOSS program?

AR 215-1.

Army Credentialing Opportunities Online (COOL)

....

TC 7-21.13, TC 7-22.7, AR 621-5

What does the acronym COOL stand for?

Army Credentialing Opportunities On-line.

Explain the COOL program?

COOL (Credentialing Opportunities On-Line) helps Army Service members find information on certifications and licenses related to their jobs and civilian careers.

What are the 4 steps in the Credentialing process?

Find & Select Related Credentials, learn about credential requirements, learn about available resources, and apply for and take the exam.

What are the types of credentials?

Licensure, Certification, and Apprenticeship.

Why are credentials important?

Civilian credentialing can contribute to military career development and may be accepted for self-development requirements and in performance evaluations. In addition, federal, state, or local law may require specific credentials to legally perform some jobs.

What regulation covers the COOL program?

AR 621-5.

Child Youth School Services (CYSS)

....

TC 7-21.13, TC 7-22.7, AR 608-10

Explain Child and Youth School Services.

CYS Services supports the Soldier which enhances Army readiness. In other words, a Soldier can concentrate on their mission knowing that their children are safe and supervised by trained and professional staff members while participating in quality developmental programs. CYSS consist of four services: Child Development Services; School Age Services; Youth Services; CYSS Liaison; and Education and Outreach Services.

What does the acronym CYSS stand for?

Child and Youth School Services.

Explain what type of program CYSS provides.

Daycare; on-line tutoring programs; and school age services.

What regulation covers CYSS?

AR 608-10.

Defense Enrollment Eligibility Reporting System (DEERS)

....

TC 7-21.13, TC 7-22.7

What does the acronym DEERS stand for?

Defense Enrollment Eligibility Reporting System.

Explain the DEERS program.

A database that contains information for each Soldier, US Sponsored foreign military, DoD and Uniformed Service civilians and other personnel and their eligible family members. It is required for TRICARE eligibility and enrollment.

Exceptional Family Member Program (EFMP)

....

TC 7-21.13, TC 7-22.7, AR 608-75

What does the acronym EFMP stand for?

Exceptional Family Member Program.

Explain the EFMP program.

A mandatory enrollment program that works with other military and civilian agencies to provide comprehensive and coordinated community support, housing, educational, medical and personnel service to families with special needs.

Do assignment managers at HRC use the EFMP program for assignment activities? Explain.

Yes, the assignment manager will look at the EFMP status and try to assign the Soldier IAW with any EFMP requirements.

What regulation covers EFMP?

AR 608-75.

Family Advocacy Program (FAP)

TC 7-21.13, TC 7-22.7, AR 608-1

What does the acronym FAP stand for?

Family Advocacy Program.

Explain the Family Advocacy Program.

It is dedicated to domestic and child abuse prevention, education, prompt reporting investigation, intervention, and treatment. Helps Soldiers and Families recognize and meet the unique challenges of military lifestyles. Services include seminars, workshops, counseling, and intervention to help strengthen Army Families, enhance resiliency and relationship skills, and improve quality of life.

What four areas does the FAP program focus on?

Personal Safety; Self Sufficiency; Personal Preparedness; and Community Cohesion.

Name 2 FAP resources?

EFMP, Transitional Compensation Program, New Parent Support, Victim Advocacy Services Program.

What regulation covers FAP?

AR 608-1.

Functional Academic Skills Training (FAST)

....

TC 7-21.13, TC 7-22.7, AR 621-5

What does the acronym FAST stand for?

Functional Academic Skills Training.

What does BSEP do?

Provides Soldiers with on-duty instruction in reading and math.

What is the goal of the BSEP program?

The goal is to improve job performance, prepare Soldiers for more advanced schooling, increase reenlistment options and enhance trainability.

What does the acronym BSEP stand for and what program is it associated with?

Basic Skills Education Program (BSEP) classes, it is part of the Functional Academic Skills Training (FAST) program.

What regulation covers the FAST program?

AR 621-5.

Name 2 of the 4 FAST programs?

BSEP, General Technical Improvement, General Education Development Test Preparation, and Reading Skill Development.

Family Readiness Group (FRG)

....

TC 7-21.13, TC 7-22.7, AR 608-1

What is the purpose of the FRG website?

A Commander's tool that allows them to communicate directly to Soldiers and Family Members. It provides all the functionality of a traditional FRG in an ad-hoc and on-line setting to meet the needs of geographically dispersed Units and Families across all components of the Army.

What does the acronym FRG stand for?

Army Family Readiness Group.

Explain the Family Readiness Group.

Army Family Readiness Group is a command sponsored organization of family members, volunteers, Soldiers and civilian employees associated with a particular unit.

What are some of the goals of an FRG?

Build Soldier and family cohesion and morale, reduce Soldier and family stress, help families become more self-sufficient, provide an avenue for sharing timely and accurate information, and to promote better use of post and community services.

What is the mission of the FRG?

(1) Act as an extension of the unit in providing official, accurate command information. (2) Provide mutual support between the command and the FRG membership. (3) Advocate more efficient use of available community resources. (4) Help Families solve problems at the lowest level.

What regulation covers the FAST program?

AR 608-1.

Family Readiness Program (FRP)

....

TC 7-21.13, TC 7-22.7, AR 608-1

What does the acronym FRP stand for?

Financial Readiness Program.

What Army Program sponsors FRP?

Army Community Services.

Explain the Financial Readiness Program.

It provides a variety of education and counseling services to assist Soldiers and Families by increasing personal readiness and reducing financial stressors.

Who is authorized to obtain services from Financial Readiness Program?

Army active duty Soldiers, and their authorized family members.

What are some of the subjects taught in the prevention education class with regard to the Financial Readiness Program?

Banking and credit union services, budget development and record keeping, credit, consumer rights and obligations, insurance, personal financial readiness, information about critical life changes such as marriage and parenthood.

What regulation covers the FRP program?

AR 608-1.

Morale Welfare Recreation (MWR)

....

TC 7-21.13, TC 7-22.7, AR 215-1

Explain the Morale Welfare and Recreation program.

A program that supports Soldiers and Families through activities and services such as: child and youth programs, recreation, sports, entertainment, travel, and leisure activities.

What does the acronym MWR stand for?

Morale, Welfare, and Recreation.

What regulation covers the MWR program?

AR 215-1.

New Parent Support Program (NPSP)

....

TC 7-21.13, AR 608-1

What does the acronym NPSP stand for?

New Parent Support Program.

Explain the NPSP program.

This voluntary participation program helps Soldiers and Family members who are expecting a child or have a child or children up to three years of age, to build strong, healthy military families. Through a variety of supportive services including home visits, support groups and parenting classes, the New Parent Support Program helps Soldiers and Families learn to cope with stress, isolation, post-deployment reunions and the everyday demands of parenthood.

What regulation covers the NPSP program?

AR 608-1.

Red Cross

....

TC 7-21.13, TC 7-22.7, AR 930-5

Explain the services of the American Red Cross.

Exists to provide compassionate care to those in need. They provide five key services: disaster relief, supporting America's Military Families; lifesaving blood, health and safety services, and international services. One of the main services the Red Cross provides is the notification to a Soldier of an emergency; such as the death or serious illness of an immediate family member.

Are Red Cross personnel subject to trail by courts-martial, if so explain?

Yes. In time of war, Red Cross personnel are subject to trial by courts-martial under the circumstances set forth in the Uniform Code of Military Justice.

What regulation covers the Red Cross program?

AR 930-5.

Soldier Family Fitness

....

TC 7-21.13, TC 7-22.7, AR 350-53

Explain the Comprehensive Soldier and Family Fitness Program/Master Resilience Trainer.

A program designed to build resilience and enhance performance of the Army Family (Soldiers, Families, and Army Civilians); provides hands on training and self-development tools so that members of the Army Family are better able to cope with adversity, perform better in stressful situations and thrive in the military and civilian sector.

What regulation covers the Comprehensive Soldier and Family Fitness program?

AR 350-53.

Soldier for Life

....

TC 7-21.13, AR 600-81

Explain the Soldier for Life-Transition Assistance Program.

The Army's transition program is responsible for providing Soldiers with counseling, employment and education workshops, and seminars.

What regulation covers the Soldier for Life program?

AR 600-81.

Tuition Assistance (TA)

....

TC 7-21.13, AR 621-5

What does the acronym TA stand for?

Tuition Assistance.

Explain Tuition Assistance.

A program which provides financial assistance for voluntary off duty civilian education in support of a Soldier's professional and personal self-development goals, allowing Soldiers to go to college.

What regulation covers the TA program?

AR 621-5.

Total Army Sponsorship Program (TASP)

....

TC 7-21.13, TC 7-22.7, AR 600-8-8

Explain the Total Army Sponsorship Program.

An important personnel function requiring command involvement. It assists Soldiers, Civilian employees, and Family members during the reassignment process by providing a sponsor to assist with settling in at a new duty station.

What does the acronym TASP stand for?

Total Army Sponsorship Program.

What regulation covers the TASP program?

AR 600-8-8.

Transitional Compensation Program (TCP)

....

TC 7-21.13, AR 608-1

What regulation covers the TCP program?

AR 608-1.

Explain the Transitional Compensation Program.

A congressionally authorized program for abused family members of military personnel. Legislation authorizes temporary monetary payments and benefits for families in which the active duty Soldier has been court-martialed with a qualifying sentence or is being administratively separated for domestic violence or a child abuse offense.

What does the acronym TCP stand for?

Transitional Compensation Program.

United Services Organization (USO)

···

TC 7-21.13, AR 930-1

What does the USO do?

Provides a friendly and safe location while waiting for connecting flights. Most have services like nurseries, snacks, beverages, games, and Wi-Fi. They also provide information on local attractions and services.

What does the acronym USO stand for?

United Services Organization.

What regulation covers the USO program?

AR 930-1.

Victim Advocacy Program (VAP)

....

TC 7-21.13, AR 608-1

Explain the Victim Advocacy Program.

Provides comprehensive assistance and support to victims of domestic abuse and sexual assault. It includes crisis intervention, safety planning, and assistance in securing medical treatment for injuries, information on legal rights and proceedings, and referral to military and civilian shelters and other resources available to victims.

What regulation covers the VAP program?

AR 608-1.

Awards

....

AR 600-8-22

What regulation covers military awards?

AR 600-8-22.

When should an award be presented to a Soldier?

Before they leave their assignment or transition from active duty.

What is the time limit for recommending an award for a Soldier?

Two years from the act or achievement.

What action is taken if a Soldier is to be presented an award, but prior to the presentation the Soldier commits an act that is not honorable?

The award will not be presented.

Under what conditions can a Soldier with a flag for overweight or a PT failure receive an award?

If the act was for valor or heroism; in addition, if a Soldier is retiring, they can receive a length of service award but it must be approved by the 1st general officer in the chain of command.

When can a Soldier receive two awards for the same act?

Never; only one decoration will be awarded to a Soldier for the same act or achievement.

When practical, how will badges be presented to the Soldier?

In a formal ceremony; however, a formal presentation is not required.

Who may recommend a Soldier for an award?

Any Soldier senior in grade to the Soldier or having first hand personal knowledge of the event may recommend the Soldier for an award.

What is the intent of the Good Conduct Medal?

To recognize selected Soldiers who distinguish themselves by exemplary conduct, efficiency, and fidelity.

The decision to award the AGCM will be based on what factors?

Commander's personal knowledge of the Soldier's individual record.

What are the normal conditions for awarding the AGCM?

Completing three continuous years of honorable service, as determined by the commander.

What does AGCM stand for?

Army Good Conduct Medal.

What is the only award that can be awarded after the mandatory 2-year period?

The Purple Heart.

What is the time limit for appealing or asking for reconsideration of a previous award recommendation?

One year from the date of the awarding authority's decision.

When does a record of non-judicial punishment disqualify a Soldier from receiving the AGCM?

It does not automatically disqualify the period of service. The commander will determine if the infraction should disqualify the period of service.

What are the types of badges?

Combat and special skill badges; Marksmanship badges; and Identification badges.

Define an impact award.

It is a rare award intended to recognize a single specific act or accomplishment. The achievement covers a short period of time with a definitive beginning and ending date.

When can a combat or special skill badge be revoked?

It will be automatically revoked on dismissal, dishonorable discharge, or conviction by courts-martial for desertion in time of war.

What action must be taken if a Soldier is disqualified from receiving an AGCM?

The unit commander will prepare a memorandum stating the rationale for their decision. The personnel office will establish a new beginning date for the next AGCM period of service.

Camouflage

STP 21-1, TC 3-21.75, FM 20-3

How should camouflage sticks be applied to exposed skin?

High shiny areas with a dark color, low shadow areas with a light color.

Define Cover.

It can be natural or manmade. It gives protection from bullets, fragments of exploding rounds, flame, nuclear effects, biological and chemical agents, and enemy observation.

Define Concealment.

Anything that hides you from enemy observation. However, it does not protect you from enemy fire.

What are the three types of cover?

Overhead, frontal, and flank/rear.

What do you do with the excess dirt when you are digging a fighting position?

Move it to the rear of the fighting position so it cannot be seen when approaching the position from the front and preferable the flank.

After a position is properly camouflaged, if you can view the position from the front at a distance of ____ meters you should not be able to see it.

35 meters or 115 feet.

How should you inspect the camouflage of your position to ensure it meets the standard?

Inspect it from the enemy's point of view from at least 35 meters or 115 feet away.

Name some examples of natural cover.

Logs, trees, reverse slope, and hollows.

CBRN

....

STP 21-1, TC 3-21.75, FM 3-11, FM 3-11.3, FM 3-11.4, FM 3-11.5

What are the core functions of CBRN?

Assess, Protect, and Mitigate.

What does WMD stand for?

Weapons of Mass Destruction.

You observe a bright flash to your immediate front, while in the open. What action should you take?

Drop to the ground, feet facing the blast, crawl to closest protection, if possible don MOPP gear, close eyes, open mouth, remain in position until wave passes and debris stops falling. Decontaminate, wash exposed skin, check for casualties, and seek shelter.

What does the acronym NBC mean?

Nuclear, Biological, and Chemical.

Describe MOPP Level 0.

All equipment and overgarments are available for immediate use.

Describe MOPP Level 1.

Worn Overgarments only. Carried: footwear cover, mask, and gloves.

Describe MOPP Level 2.

Worn Overgarments and footwear cover. Carried: Mask and Gloves.

Describe MOPP Level 3.

Worn Overgarments, footwear covers, mask and hood. Carried: Gloves.

Describe MOPP Level 4.

Worn: Overgarments, footwear covers, mask and hood, and gloves.

What does the acronym CBRN stand for?

Chemical, Biological, Radiological or Nuclear Weapons.

Name three CBRN threats.

Chemical, Biological, Nuclear, WMD, Improvised CBRN devices.

What are the four levels of decontamination?

Immediate, operational, thorough, and clearance.

What is a CBRN 1 report?

Observer's initial report.

What are the three fundamentals of CBRN defense?

Contamination avoidance, protection, and decontamination.

What is the STRIKWARN system used for?

A system for the warning of friendly nuclear strikes.

What are the three methods used to warn of a CBRN attack?

Vocal, Sound, Visual.

What is your unit's Sound method to indicate a CBRN attack?

_____{Insert Unit Procedure}.

What are the types of Biological Agents?

Pathogens and Toxins.

Name 5 symptoms of exposure to a Biological Agent?

Dizziness, mental confusion, double or blurred vision, skin tingling, numbness, paralysis, convulsions, rashes, blisters, coughing, fever, aching muscles, fatigue, difficulty swallowing, nausea, vomiting, and/or diarrhea.

What action should a leader take before selecting an individual for unmasking procedures?

Secure their weapon.

What is the purpose of the M291 Decontamination Kit?

Decontamination of the skin through physical removal, absorption, or neutralization of toxic agents.

What is the purpose of the M295 Decontamination Kit?

Decontamination of individual equipment through physical removal, and absorption of chemical agents.

What is the SDS M100 used for?

It replaces the M11 and M13s systems for the operator to spray down critical parts of their equipment.

What is M8 paper used for?

Detecting liquid V type nerve, G type nerve and H type blister agents.

Describe the color M8 paper will turn for each type of agent.

V type nerve agent: dark green, G type nerve agent: yellow, H type blister agent: red.

What is M9 paper used for?

It is placed on personnel and equipment to identify the presence of liquid chemical agent aerosols.

What type of agents does M9 paper detect, and what colors will it turn?

Liquid agents: pink, red, reddish brown, or red purple.

What is the M256 Kit used for?

A portable and expendable kit that is capable of detecting and identifying hazardous concentrations of chemical agents.

What is the NAAK Mark I Kit used for?

Immediate first aid treatment. It contains one small autoinjector of atropine and a second autoinjector of pralidoxime chloride.

What is NAPP used for?

It is an investigative new nerve agent, pretreatment drug which requires presidential approval for use by military personnel.

What is the CANA used for?

A convulsant antidote for nerve agents. The auto injectors contain diazepam.

What is SERPACWA used for?

Skin Exposure Reduction Paste Against Chemical Warfare Agents is used as a topical skin protectant to protect personnel from penetration or absorption of vapor or liquid CB agents.

What is the difference between a persistent and non-persistent agent?

Non-persistent remains in the area for no more than 15 minutes while a persistent agent can last longer than 24 hours.

In what methods can chemical weapons be deployed?

Bombs, rockets, mines, aerosols, gas, liquid, and vapor.

What are four types of chemical agents?

Blood, Blister, Choking, and Nerve.

Code of Conduct

The Code of Conduct consists of how many articles?

6.

What is the 1st article of the code of conduct?

I am an American fighting in the forces which guard my country and our way of life. I am prepared to give my life in their defense.

What is the 2nd article of the code of conduct?

I will never surrender of my own free will. If in command, I will never surrender the members of my command while they still have the means to resist.

What is the 3rd article of the code of conduct?

If I am captured, I will continue to resist by all means available. I will make every effort to escape and aid others to escape. I will accept neither parole nor special favors from the enemy.

What is the 4th article of the code of conduct?

If I become a prisoner of war, I will keep faith with my fellow prisoners. I will give no information or take part in any action which might be harmful to my comrades. If I am senior, I will take command. If not, I will obey the lawful orders of those appointed over me and will back them up in every way.

What is the 5th article of the code of conduct?

When questioned, should I become a prisoner of war, I am required to give only my name, rank, service number, and date of birth. I will evade answering further questions to the utmost of my ability. I will make no oral or written statement disloyal to my country and its allies or harmful to their cause.

What is the 6th article of the code of conduct?

I will never forget that I am an American fighting for freedom, responsible for my actions, and dedicated to the principles which made my country free. I will trust in my God and in the United States of America.

How should prisoners be separated?

Officers, NCOs, Enlisted, females and civilians.

What President enacted the code of conduct?

Dwight Eisenhower.

How was the code of conduct enacted?

By executive order 10631.

When was the code of conduct enacted?

17 August 1955.

When was the code of conduct modified?

1988.

What was a major achievement of the Geneva Convention of 1949?

It provided for specific protection of POWs, WIAs, and civilians in a war zone.

Cold Weather Operations

··

TC 21-3

What manual covers cold weather operations?

TC 21-3.

What subject does TC 21 -3 cover?

Cold weather operations.

What does the acronym COLD stand for?

Keep it clean, avoid overheating, wear it loose, and keep it dry.

Soldiers should avoid wearing what type of clothing in cold weather?

Tight and/or dirty clothing.

When Soldiers withdraw and do not want to leave the comfort and protection of a warm shelter, what is the best remedy?

Soldiers should do physical activity and remain alert and active.

What are the keys to staying warm?

Keeping the body clean, dry, and warm; ensuring proper rest and nourishment are vital.

What are the four rules for staying warm?

Keep in shape; drink plenty of water; eat to keep fit; and maintain a good attitude.

Which method of dressing provides the best insulation: one heavy cold weather garment or several layers of clothing?

Several layers of clothing provide more insulation.

Eating snow is not a good water substitute because?

It will lower your core body temperature.

What is another name for trench foot?

Immersion foot.

How do you dry wet socks and other clothing?

Socks are best dried by placing them against your body. Other pieces of clothing can be dried by hanging them on the outside of your rucksack during movement.

How much water should you drink a day to avoid dehydration?

3.5 quarts per day.

Command Policy

Breast Feeding

....

AR 600-20

If a Soldier wants to breastfeed their child upon return to duty what action must a take?

Notified their chain of command as soon as possible.

How long must a commander allow the Soldier breast feeding breaks?

At least one year after the child's birth.

If a Soldier is in field training and cannot express breast milk for transportation to garrison, what action will a commander take?

The commander will permit the Soldier the same time and space to express and discard milk with the intent to maintain physiological capability for lactation.

Bullying

AR 600-20

Define bullying.

A form of harassment that includes acts of aggression by Soldiers or DA Civilian employees, with a nexus to military service, with the intent of harming a Soldier either physically or psychologically, without proper military authority or other governmental purpose

Soldiers who bully or haze other Soldiers are subject to what type of action?

Punishment under the UCMJ as determined by the commander.

Which act, bullying or hazing, takes the form of excessive corrective measures?

Bullying.

What type of behavior best describes the following event? A Soldier new to the unit is not being welcomed into the squad because an informal leader is spreading rumors about the Soldier and isolating the Soldier from involvement with the squad.

Bullying best describes this activity.

Chain of Command

AR 600-20

Define Chain of Command.

The sequence of commanders in an organization who have direct authority and primary responsibility for accomplishing the assigned unit mission while caring for personnel and property in their charge.

What does AR 600-20 state with regard to using of the chain of command?

Soldiers WILL use the chain of command when communicating issues and problems to their leaders and commanders.

What regulation covers Army Command Policy and Procedure?

AR 600-20.

How is seniority determined among enlisted members when they are of the same rank?

First by date of rank; when date of rank is the same then by total length of active federal service; If both date of rank and active federal service are the same then seniority will be determined by date of birth.

Name the Commander in Chief (President)

_____

Name the Secretary of Defense

_____

Name the Secretary of the Army

_____

Name the Army Chief of Staff

_____

Name your Division Commander

_____

Name your Brigade Commander

_____

Name your Company/Battery/Troop Commander

_____

Name your Platoon Leader

_____

Name your Squad Leader

_____

Name your Team Leader

_____

Corrective Training

....

AR 600-20, FM 7-22, AR 27-10

An on-the-spot correction is an example of what type of action?

It is an example of administrative corrective measures or corrective training.

What other names is corrective training referred to as?

Extra training or extra instruction.

What Army Regulations cover corrective training?

AR 600-20 and AR 27-10.

What are nonpunitive corrective measures

They are the primary tools for teaching proper standards of conduct and performance.

When due nonpunitive corrective measures constitute punishment?

These measures never constitute punishment. Punishment is given under UCMJ actions.

Counseling

....

AR 600-20, ATP 6-22.1, AR 350-1, AR 623-3, AR 635-200

What are the performance counseling requirements for PVT-SPC?

There are no specific counseling requirements for these grades. Commander will determine the timing and specific methods used to provide guidance and direction to these Soldiers through counseling.

What ATP covers the Counseling Process?

ATP 6 - 22.1.

What type of counseling occurs when issues are beyond the expertise of the chain of command?

Referral Counseling.

What are the four stages of the counseling process?

1. Identify the need
2. Prepare for counseling
3. Conduct the counseling
4. Follow-up

What are the three major categories of Developmental Counseling?

Event
Performance
Professional Growth Counseling.

What is the disadvantage of the nondirective approach?

More time consuming and requires a high degree of counseling skill.

What is the quickest method of counseling?

Directive.

What regulation covers adverse separation counseling?

AR 635-200.

What are the four stages of conducting the counseling session?

1.   Open the session
2.   Discuss the issues
3.   Develop a plan of action
4.   Record and close the session

Name the seven steps in preparing for a counseling session?

1.   Select a suitable place
2.   Schedule the time
3.   Notify the Soldier in advance
4.   Outline the session
5.   Organize information and draft a plan of action
6.   Plan the counseling strategy
7.   Establish the right atmosphere.

In what stage of the counseling session does the leader state the purpose and establish the setting of the counseling?

Opening the session.

Developmental counseling may not apply during what types of situations?

Serious Acts of Misconduct.

When should a Soldier expect to receive their initial counseling upon arriving at their duty station?

Within 30 days of arrival.

What will proper counseling identify?

Proper counseling will identify individual strengths, weaknesses, and developmental needs.

According to AR 635-200, what must be done before initiating separation proceedings against a Soldier?

Diligent efforts will be made to identify Soldiers who exhibit a likelihood for early separation and to improve their chances for retention through counseling, retraining, and rehabilitation prior to initiation of separation proceedings.

Criminal Self Reporting & Convictions

AR 600-20

Name three actions a commander can take with regard to a Soldier's career, if the Solider has a conviction under US criminal law?

1. Commanders may consider the conviction for inclusion in evaluation reports
2. Future assignments
3. Selection for schools
4. Awards
5. Initiation of separation and suspension of security clearance. This is not a complete list.
6. Access to government-owned IT systems

How long does a Soldier have to report a conviction under U. S. criminal law?

Within 15 days of the conviction.

What action must a Soldier in the grade of E-6 or above take if they are convicted of a violation of U. S. criminal law?

They MUST self-report the conviction to the chain of command.

Domestic Violence

AR 600-20

What is the Lautenberg Amendment?

A legislative act that makes it unlawful for any person to transfer, issue, sell or otherwise dispose of firearms or ammunition to any person whom they know or has reasonable cause to believe the individual has been convicted of a misdemeanor crime of domestic violence.

What action must a Soldier take if they obtain a qualifying conviction for domestic violence?

They MUST notify their commander or supervisor of the conviction.

What action will a commander take with regard to reenlistment, when a Soldier has a qualifying domestic violence condition?

The Soldier will be barred from reenlistment.

How long may a Soldier with a qualifying domestic violence conviction be allowed to remain in service?

Up to 12 months from the date HQDA is notified of the qualifying conviction.

What type of position or duty will a Soldier with a qualifying conviction for domestic violence be assigned?

Meaningful duties that do not require access to weapons or ammunition.

Commanders must take what action when a soldier has a qualifying conviction for domestic violence?

They must flagged the soldier in accordance with AR 600-8-2.

Equal Opportunity

....

AR 600-20, TC 7-21.13
What does MEO stand for?

Military Equal Opportunity.

What regulation covers the Army equal opportunity program?

AR 600-20.

Explain the EO program.

Provides fair treatment for military personnel and family members without regard to race, color, gender, religion, national origin, sexual orientation, and provides an environment free of unlawful discrimination and offensive behavior.

Define discrimination.

An act that unlawfully or unjustly results in unequal treatment of persons or groups based on race, color, gender, national origin, or religion.

How long does an individual have to make and EO complaint?

60 calendar days from the date of the incident for a formal complaint.

Who is your unit Equal Opportunity Representative?

_____

Who is your unit Equal Opportunity Advisor?

_____

What are the three methods available to report or process an EO Complaint?

Anonymous, formal, and informal.

Evaluations

....

AR 600-20, AR 623-3, DA PAM 623-3

What regulation covers the evaluation reporting system?

AR 623-3.

How will the rating chain be structured?

They will correspond with the chain of command or chain of supervision.

What support forms will a Soldier receive at the beginning of the rated period?

A copy of the rater's and senior rater's support form.

When will an initial NCOER counseling be conducted?

Within 30 days of the start of the rating.

Who will normally be appointed a Soldier's rater?

The immediate supervisor.

How many days of observation must a Senior Rater have to rate a Soldier?

A minimum of 60 calendar days.

What document tell a rated Soldier who their supplementary reviewer is?

The published rating scheme.

What is the normal minimum rating period for an evaluation report?

90 days.

What form is used to document the initial and quarterly counseling sessions for an NCOER?

DA FORM 2166-9-1A.

What are the two types of evaluation reports?

Mandatory and optional.

What documents does the rated Soldier use when developing goals and objectives?

The rater and senior rater support forms.

How will the rated NCO verify the face-to-face counseling sessions with the rater?

By dating and initialing the support form or the DA Form 2166-9-1A.

How often will follow-up counseling be conducted?

Quarterly.

How does the senior rater verify the face-to-face counseling has taken place with the rated NCO?

By dating and initialing the support form.

What chapter of AR 623-3 covers the appeal process?

Chapter 4.

What is the purpose of the commander's inquiry?

It provides a greater degree of command involvement and prevents injustices and corrects errors before the report becomes a matter of permanent record.

Who has access to evaluation reports?

The rating chain, the rated Soldier, and those that process the report.

What is a commander's inquiry?

An investigation into a Soldier's evaluation report made by an official in the chain of command to determine if something in the report is illegal, unjust, or in violation of regulation.

What is a rater tendency report?

A document provided by HQDA for raters of NCOs. It shows the rater's rating assessment history, by grade of previous NCOs rated.

What is redress?

The process by which a Soldier can address errors, bias, or injustices during and after the preparation of an evaluation report and have them corrected.

Who conducts an undocumented review of the evaluation report?

The 1SG, SGM, or CSM.

What is the purpose of the DA form 2166-9-1A?

This form assures a verified communication process for the rating period.

Can the failure to use a support form or failure to counsel be the basis for an appeal?

Yes, it can be a basis for appeal, but it cannot be the sole reason for the appeal.

How does the rater determine the overall performance of the rated NCO for the rating period?

This performance is evaluated in terms of the rated NCO's performance compared against other NCOs of the same rank that the rater is currently or has previously rated.

What is the maximum percentage of "Most Qualified" ratings a senior rater can have for NCOs?

24% or less.

What achievement or comments from an academic evaluation report can be entered on an NCOER?

No comments from an academic evaluation report may be entered on a NCOER.

Can comments about a Soldier's marital status and/or spouse be mentioned in an evaluation report?

Yes. but only in rare occasions when necessary to properly evaluate the rated Soldier's performance and potential.

If a Soldier voluntarily enters the ASAP program for a situation not detected by the chain of command, what comments will be placed on the rated Soldiers evaluation report?

No comment will be placed on the evaluation report. The Soldier will not be penalized by mentioning participation in the ASAP program if they voluntarily entered the program and the condition was not detected by the chain of command.

How long does a Soldier have to submit an evaluation appeal?

Substantiated appeals must be submitted within three years of an evaluation report "thru" date.

If a rated Soldier has 60 days rated time and 30 days nonrated time can they receive an evaluation report? Explain

No, the Soldier must have 90 days of rated time. The 30 days nonrated time cannot be counted towards the 90-day rating period.

What performance or incidents will not be contained in an evaluation report?

No performance or incidents will be included in an evaluation report where the issue occurred either before the rating period, after the rating period, or during periods of non-rated time.

If an acronym is not found in the authorized abbreviation, brevity codes, and acronym database how is the acronym written in a NCOER evaluation report?

The abbreviation or acronym must be spelled out completely the first time it is used. The abbreviation is then entered in parentheses immediately after the spelled-out version. After this is completed abbreviation may be used throughout the evaluation report.

What type of comment can be placed on an evaluation report if a Soldier complains to a member of the United States Congress?

No comment can be placed on the Soldier's evaluation report because it's considered protected communication.

Extremists Activity

....

AR 600-20

What actions can a commander take if a Soldier is participating in extremist activities?

They can consider punishment under Articles 92, 116, 117, 134 of the UCMJ, involuntary separation, bar to reenlistment, and/or other administrative or disciplinary actions.

Give two examples that the chain of command can use to determine participation in criminal gangs?

1. Wearing of gang colors or clothing; tattoos or body markings associated with criminal gangs
2. Slogan
3. Graffiti
4. Clothing style or color
5. Activities furthering the objectives of gang organizations detrimental to the good order, discipline, or mission accomplishment is incompatible with military service

How can an individual report suspected extremists activity?

Chain of command, anonymous calls.

Family Care Plans
....

AR 600-20

What regulation covers Family Care Plans?

AR 600-20.

Name three conditions in which a Family Care Plan must be prepared.

1. Pregnancy
2. Soldier has minor dependents and is either divorced, widowed, separated, not residing with their spouse, married to another service member
3. A family member incapable of self-care
4. Or a Soldier that bears the sole responsibility for the care of a child under the age of 18.

How long does a Soldier have to complete a valid family care plan?

30 days with an optional extension by the commander of another 30 days.

How often are family care plans recertified?

At least annually.

If a pregnant Soldier does not have a spouse; is divorced, widowed, separated, is married to another service member or residing without a spouse what action must they take?

They must have a family care plan.

If parenthood interferes with military responsibilities what action will the command take?

The Soldier will be counseled on voluntary and involuntary separation.

When should a pregnant Soldier be counseled on family care plan requirements?

As soon as the pregnancy is identified but no later than 90 days prior to the expected date of birth.

Who is the sole approving authority of the DA Form 5305?

The unit commander.

What is the deployable status of a Soldier without a family care plan?

They are nondeployable.

Finance

....

AR 600-20, AR 37-104-4

What is the primary regulation that covers the military policy on pay and allowances?

AR 37-104-4.

What report does the commander review on a monthly basis concerning financial entitlement?

The Unit Commander's Finance Report (UCFR).

What does the acronym BAS stand for?

Basic Allowance for Subsistence.

What does the acronym RIKNA stand for?

Rations in kind not available.

When is an advance in pay authorized?

1. PCS
2. Evacuation of member or dependents
3. Advance of allotments to dependents
4. Advance for members of the Armed Forces Health Profession Scholarship Program
5. Advance of BAH
6. Advance of BAS only when an enlisted Soldier is ordered to a remote location where mess is not readily available
7. Advance pay for Senior Reserve Officers' Training Corps.

Give two examples of informal unit funds a commander may authorize.

1. Office Coffee
2. Cup and Flower
3. Annual Picnic funds

What action can a commander take if the soldier fails to settle their financial accounts before PCSing?

They may consider punishment under UCMJ.

Hazing

....

AR 600-20

A Soldier successfully graduates Airborne School and receives blood wings from the squad. The Soldier is fine with the activity. This would be an example of what type of behavior and is it acceptable because the Soldier approved of the ritual?

This is an example of Hazing. Even if the Soldier approves of the ritual it is still in violation of Army policy.

Typically hazing is normally directed at individuals who have recently ___?

Achieved a career milestone.

Define hazing.

A form of harassment that includes conduct through which Soldiers or DA Civilian employees (who haze Soldiers), without a proper military authority or other governmental purpose but with a nexus to military service, physically or psychologically injures or creates a risk of physical or psychological injury to Soldiers for the purpose of: initiation into, admission into, affiliation with, change in status or position within, or a condition for continued membership in any military or DA Civilian organization.

What actions, when authorized by the chain of command, DO NOT constitute hazing or bullying?

1. Physical and mental hardships associated with operations and training
2. Lawful punishment imposed under UCMJ
3. Administrative corrective measures
4. Valid corrective training
5. Physical training
6. Other similar activities authorized by the chain of command

Where can a Soldier who is being exposed to hazing or bullying make an official complaint?

1. The chain of command
2. Commander
3. Law enforcement
4. The IG

When is an act of hazing most likely to occur?

During a rite of passage or congratulatory act.

Name four acts of conduct that are normally involved with hazing.

1. Any form of initiation or congratulatory act that involves physically striking, beating, paddling, whipping, or burning another person in any manner or threatening to do the same; Pressing any object into another person's skin, regardless of whether it pierces the skin, such as "pinning" or "tacking on" of rank insignia, aviator wings, jump wings, diver insignia, badges, medals, or any other object;
2. Oral or written berating of another person with the purpose of belittling or humiliating;
3. Encouraging another person to engage in illegal, harmful, demeaning, or dangerous acts;
4. Playing abusive or malicious tricks;
5. Excessive physical exercise;
6. Confinement to restricted areas, isolation, or sleep-deprivation;
7. Immersion in noxious substances;
8. Branding, handcuffing, duct taping, tattooing, shaving, greasing, or painting another person;
9. Subjecting another person to excessive or abusive use of water; and
10. Forcing another person to consume food, alcohol, drugs, or any other substance.

Can subordinates haze or bully a superior?

Yes.

What standard is used to determine if an activity is hazing?

The reasonable person rule.

How can an electronic communication be used to inflict harm?

By sharing or posting signs, writing, images, sounds, or data.

Informal Funds

....

AR 600-20

Commanders may authorize informal funds, provide two examples.

Office coffee cup funds, cup and flower, and annual picnic bonds.

What expenses may be taken from an informal fund?

Only expenses consistent with the purpose and function of the fund.

How many people must be responsible for the custody, accounting and documentation of the fund?

This responsibility must be held by only one person.

When should raising money four and formal bonds be curtailed?

When such efforts might interfere or compete with CFC or AER campaign

Language Policy

....

AR 600-20

What language is considered the operational language of the Army?

English.

What are the language requirements for a Soldier in the US Army?

They must maintain sufficient proficiency of the English language to perform their military duties.

Can commanders order or require Soldiers speak English in the performance of their military duties?

Yes, the commander can order such action if it is necessary for proper performance of MILITARY functions.

Medical Care

....

AR 600-20

If a Soldier refuses to take immunizations what action can be taken against the Soldier?

They can be punished under UCMJ and/or administrative action can be taken against the Solider for failure to obey a lawful order.

What action can be taken if a Soldier refuses medical treatment required to save their life, health, or fitness for duty?

If the unit commander is not available, the hospital commander may order the treatment.

What action, other than UCMJ, can be taken against a Soldier who refuses to submit to medical care or refuses to submit to dental care and/or dental X-rays?

The Soldier WILL BE referred to a medical board.

What action may be taken against a Soldier who refuses immunizations?

Under certain conditions they can be involuntarily administered immunizations.

Military Discipline and Conduct

AR 600-20

How is military authority to be exercised?

Promptly, firmly, courteously and fairly.

What regulation covers military discipline and conduct?

AR 600-20.

How are Soldiers expected to obey orders?

They are required to strictly obey and promptly execute legal orders of their lawful seniors.

What is considered one of the most effective administrative corrective measures?

Corrective training also known as extra training or instruction, including on the spot corrections.

When you are speaking about a Command Sergeant Major, Sergeant, Sergeant First Class or Major General, (etc.), to another person how do you address them by rank?

You would state the entire rank to ensure there is no confusion. For example, you would say something like "Command Sergeant Major Davis, Sergeant Davis, Sergeant First Class Davis, or Major General Davis." This ensures the other person understands the rank of the person being discussed.

What courtesies should the rendered by Soldiers to the national anthem and national colors?

Soldier should render proper respect while on duty or off duty, in uniform morale uniform.

NCO Support Channel

....

AR 600-20, TC 7-21.13

Define the NCO support channel.

It parallels and complements the chain of command. It is a channel of communication and supervision from the CSM to the 1SG and then to other NCOs and enlisted personnel of the unit.

When is an NCO or enlisted Soldier allowed or required to assume command of a unit?

In the absence or disability of all officers in the unit. Pending the assignment and arrival of the new commander, the enlisted person will exercise temporary command of the unit.

Does an NCO participate in work details other than supervisory duties?

Function only in supervisory roles on work details and only as NCOs of the guard on guard duty, except when temporary personnel shortages require the NCO to actively participate in the work detail.

Name the Sergeant Major of the Army

Name the Corps CSM

Name your Division CSM

Name your Brigade CSM

Name your Battalion CSM

Name your First Sergeant

Name your Squad/Section Leader

Open Door Policy

AR 600-20

If a Soldier uses the open-door policy, can they receive an Article 15 for failing to use the chain of command? Explain.

No; While using the chain of command is specifically preferred. AR 600-20 directs commanders at all levels to have an open-door policy and a Soldier cannot be prevented from seeing a commander or other senior enlisted leader to communicate a problem or issue. In these situations, the first line leaders should attempt to determine why the Soldier did not feel comfortable discussing the issue with the first line leader.

Discuss the commander's open-door policy requirements.

Commanders will ensure they establish an open-door policy. The timing, conduct and specific procedures of this policy are determined by the commander.

Ready and Resilient Campaign

....

AR 600-20

What does the acronym CR2C stand for?

Commander's Ready and Resilient Campaign.

The act of help-seeking behavior falls under what program?

Ready and Resilient Campaign.

With regard to the CR2C program, what are the commander and leaders required to provide?

A positive environment that contributes positively to the mental, physical, spiritual, and emotional dimensions of the lives of their subordinates and their families.

Name two of the four strategic objectives of the ready and resilient campaign.

1. Sustained personal readiness to meet operational requirements.
2. Sustain a values-based organization of trusted Army professionals.
3. Enhanced visibility of personal readiness throughout a career.
4. R2 management that enables personal readiness.

Relationships

....

AR 600-20

Relationships between Soldiers of different ranks cannot be or perceived to exhibit _____.

Familiarity.

Provide two examples of behavior that could be considered as an inappropriate relationship between Soldiers of different ranks (actual or perceived).

Repeated visits to bars, nightclubs, eating establishments, or homes.

What types of gatherings between Soldiers of different ranks are permitted and would not violate the policies of AR 600-20 concerning relationships?

Social gatherings that involve the entire unit, office, or work section.

Who is held accountable for participating in an inappropriate relationship between Soldiers of different ranks?

All members of the relationship are held accountable.

What is the exception to the sharing of living accommodations rule between Soldiers of different ranks IAW AR 600-20?

Shared living accommodations between Soldiers of different ranks are authorized for operational requirements.

If two Soldiers of the same rank are dating and one of the Soldiers is commissioned as an officer, is this relationship compliant with AR 600-20? Explain.

No, once a change in status occurs, the relationship is in violation of AR 600-20. The Soldiers must either terminate the relationship or marry within one year of the change of status.

Religion

....

AR 600-20

Who is the approving authority for accommodation of religious practices that do not require a wavier?

The unit commander.

What action can a commander grant for individuals who desire to observe lengthy holy periods?

They may grant ordinary leave.

What restrictions are placed on religious apparel while in uniform?

They cannot interfere with military duties or interfere with the proper wearing of any authorized article of the uniform.

How will all requests for accommodation religious practices?

On a case-by-case basis.

Sexual Harassment

AR 600-20

What regulation covers prevention of sexual harassment?

AR 600-20.

What is the Army policy on sexual harassment?

The Army does not tolerate or condone sexual harassment, sexual assault, or associated retaliatory behaviors.

What are the categories of sexual harassment?

1. Verbal
2. Nonverbal
3. Physical contact

Define sexual harassment.

Conduct that involves unwelcome sexual advances, requests for sexual favors, and deliberate or repeated offensive comments of a general nature.

Using terms such as honey, babe, sweetheart, dear, stud, or hunk would be considered what type of sexual harassment?

Verbal.

What type of sexual harassment involves the action of undressing someone with your eyes, blowing kisses, winking, or licking one's lips in a suggestive manner?

Nonverbal.

The following actions constitute what type of sexual harassment touching, patting, pinching, bumping, grabbing, cornering, blocking a passageway, kissing, or providing unsolicited back or neck rubs?

Physical.

SHARP

AR 600-20, TC 7-21.13

What regulation covers sexual assault prevention and response prevention program?

AR 600-20.

What does the acronym SHARP stand for?

Sexual Assault Prevention and Response Prevention.

How long does a Soldier with knowledge of a sexual assault have to report the incident?

24 hours.

What type of offense is sexual assault?

It is a criminal offense.

What does the acronym SARC stand for?

Sexual Assault Response Coordinator.

What action will a SARC take if a victim chooses restricted reporting?

The victim will be taken to a healthcare provider in lieu of reporting the incident to law enforcement or the command.

What does SHARP VA stand for?

Sexual Harassment/Assault Response and Prevention Victim Advocate.

What does SHARP VR stand for?

Sexual Harassment/Assault Response and Prevention Victim Representative.

Who is your unit SHARP representative?

Who is your is your Military Equal Opportunity Representative?

Travel Card

AR 600-20

Define misuse of a government travel card.

Misuse of a government charge card includes any improper or fraudulent use of a government travel charge card, including any use at establishments or for purposes that are inconsistent with the official business of the Army or with applicable standards of conduct.

In what type of situations would the use of a government travel card be considered misuse?

Any improper or fraudulent use including use at an establishment or for purposes inconsistent with the official business of the Army or with applicable standards of conduct. For example: expenses related to adult entertainment and gambling.

What options are available to the commander for Soldiers that abuse or misuse the government travel card?

Corrective and disciplinary action including punishment under the UCMJ.

What expenses can the travel card be used for in a travel status?

Non-reimbursable incidental travel expenses, such as rental movies, personal telephone calls, exercise fees, and beverages, when these charges are part of a room billing or meal and are reasonable.

How are non-reimburseable personal expenses paid with regard to the Government Travel Card?

The traveler will pay for incidental non-reimbursable personal expenses as part of the normal billing process.

Unit Memorial Services

AR 600-20

What is the purpose of unit memorial ceremonies and services?

To show respect for the service of the Soldiers who have died and to offer support to unit survivors.

Unit memorials ceremonies will be conducted for which member of the unit?

All members of the unit for every Soldier who dies while assigned to their unit, regardless of the manner of death to include suicides.

When can commander the request an exception to policy NOT to conduct a ceremony?

When the deceased Soldier has been convicted of a capital offense under Federal or State law in which the person was sentenced to death or life imprisonment without parole or convicted of serious offense or when the ceremony would bring discredit upon the Army.

Who must approve the exception not to conduct a ceremony?

The first GO in the chain of command.

Communications

....

TC 3-21.75, TC 3-21-.76

What is the most secured means of communications?

Messenger.

What is the precedence of reporting on a radio net?

Flash, Immediate, Priority, Routine.

When is "FLASH" radio traffic used?

To report initial enemy contact reports.

What is an SOI?

Signal Operating Instructions.

What are the methods of communication?

Messenger, Radio, Visual, Wire, and Sound.

Drill and Ceremony

TC 7-22.7, TC 3-21.5

What is the purpose of Drill?

Drill enables commanders to quickly move their forces from one point to another, mask their forces into a battle formation that affords maximum firepower, and maneuver those forces as the situation develops.

What subject matter does TC 3-21.5 cover?

Drill and ceremony.

Who created the first manual for drill used by the US Army?

Baron Friedrich Von Stuben.

What was the first manual for drill referred to as or called?

The blue book.

To revoke a preparatory command what is the command?

As You Were.

In regard to drill and ceremony, what is alignment?

The arrangement of several elements on the same line.

In regard to drill and ceremony, what is cover?

Aligning oneself directly behind the person to one's immediate front while maintaining correct distance.

In regard to drill and ceremony, what is distance?

The space between elements when the elements are one behind the other. Between units, it varies with the size of the formation; between Soldiers it is an arm's length to the front plus six inches or about 36 inches, measured from the chest of one Soldier to the back of the Soldier immediately in front.

In regard to drill and ceremony, define an element.

An individual, squad, section, platoon, company, or larger unit forming the part of the next higher unit.

In regard to drill and ceremony, what is a file?

A column that has a front of one element.

What is a flank?

The right or left side of any formation as observed by an element within that formation.

What is a formation?

The arrangement of elements of a unit in a prescribed manner.

In regard to drill and ceremony, what is a line?

A formation in which the elements are side by side or abreast of each other.

In regard to drill and ceremony, what is a column?

A formation in which the elements are one behind the other.

How do you change a line formation to a column formation?

To change a line formation to a column formation, the command is Right Face. To change a column formation to a line formation, the command is Left Face.

How do you change a column formation to a line formation?

To change a column formation to a line formation, the command is Left Face.

In regard to drill and ceremony, what is a front?

The space from side to side of a formation, including the right and left elements.

In regard to drill and ceremony, what is the guide?

The person responsible for maintaining the prescribed direction and rate of march.

How many types of interval are there?

Three.

What are the 3 types of interval?

Close interval; double interval; and normal interval.

What is close interval?

Lateral space between Soldiers, measured from right to left by the Soldier on the right placing the heel of the left hand on the hip, even with the top of the belt line, fingers and thumb extended and joined downward, with the elbow in line with the body and touching the arm of the Soldier to their left.

What is double interval?

Lateral space between Soldiers, measured from right to left by raising both arms shoulder high with fingers extended and joined (palms down) so that the fingertips are touching the fingertips of the Soldier to the right and left.

What is normal interval?

Lateral space between Soldiers, measured from right to left by the Soldier on the right holding their left arm shoulder high, fingers and thumb extended and joined, with the tip of the middle finger touching the right shoulder of the Soldier to their left.

In regard to drill and ceremony, what is post?

The correct place for an officer or noncommissioned officer to stand in a prescribed formation.

What is a step?

The prescribed distance measured from one heel to the other heel of the marching Soldier.

What is a two-part command?

A command having a preparatory command and a command of execution. For example: Right Face.

What is a combined command?

The preparatory command and the command of execution are combined. For example, FALL IN.

What is a supplementary command?

Oral orders given by a subordinate leader that reinforces and complements a commander's order.

How did the hand salute originate?

The salute dates back to Roman times and the age of the knights. When knights would approach one another in peace they would raise their visor with their right hand. The tradition has evolved into the hand salute.

Name the instructional methods for conducting drill and ceremony.

Step by step, talk through, and by the numbers.

How many types of commands are there?

Four.

What are the four types of commands?

Two part, directives, supplementary, and combined.

How many rest positions are there and name them?

Four. Rest, Parade Rest, Stand at Ease, At Ease.

When do Soldiers take 15-inch steps?

Left Step, Right Step, Backwards Step, and Half Step.

When marching on what foot should a command be given?

If the movement is to the right, the command is given as the right foot strikes the ground; if the movement is to the left the command is given on the left foot as it strikes the ground.

When given the command Rest, what may a Soldier do?

They may move, talk, smoke, drink unless otherwise directed but must remain standing with the right foot in place.

Who initiates a salute?

The subordinate.

How many steps per minute is quick time march?

120 steps per minute.

What is the length of a marching step?

30 inches.

How many steps per minute is double time march?

180 steps per minute.

On what foot is the command Change Step, March given?

Right foot.

On what foot is the command Mark Time March given?

Either foot.

What is the approximate distance in which a Soldier should salute?

Approximately six paces.

When is a salute terminated?

Upon acknowledgment.

What takes place when the platoon is given the command Open Ranks March?

1st squad takes two steps forward; 2nd squad takes one step forward; 3rd rank stands fast; 4th rank takes two backward steps; 5th rank would take four steps back; etc.

When boarding Navy ships what must a Soldier do?

At the top of the gangway, face and salute the national ensign. Turn and salute the officer of the deck and state: "Sir Request permission to come aboard."

Enlisted Separations

AR 635-200

What does AR 635-200 cover?

Active Duty Enlisted Administration Separations.

Why should every means to rehabilitate a Soldier be taken before a Separation action is initiated?

Because the Army makes a substantial investment in training, time, equipment and related expenses when a person enters military service; therefore, it is considered wasteful and results in loss of investment and generates a required increase for accessions.

If a Soldier is identified for potential Separation, what actions should normally be taken prior to initiating separation?

Attempt to correct substandard performance or behavior using corrective training, counseling, retraining, and rehabilitation.

Give an example of when separation is warranted and counseling/rehabilitative measures are not required.

When a Soldier commits a serious offense, a Soldier may be separated without these measures.

What are the requirements to separate a Soldier?

The Soldier must be formally notified of their deficiencies. At least one formal counseling session is required before separation proceedings are initiated. There must also be evidence that the deficiencies continued after the initial formal counseling.

Can a Soldier be processed for separation and the separation action be suspended (similar to suspended punishment under an Article 15)? If so explain.

Yes; a highly deserving Soldier may be given a probation period to show successful rehabilitation before the Soldier's enlistment or obligated service expires; the probation will not exceed 12 months.

When is a Bad Conduct Discharge given?

Pursuant only to an approved sentence of a general court-martial or special court-martial.

If a Soldier is an Alcohol or Drug Abuse Rehabilitation Failure, under which chapter of AR 635-200 will they be separated?

Chapter 9.

Under what chapter of AR 635-200 will a Soldier with Unsatisfactory Performance be separated?

Chapter 13.

Under what chapter of AR 635-200 will a Soldier be separated for Failure to Meet Weight Standards?

Chapter 18.

If a Solider is separated due to a personality disorder which chapter is used?

Chapter 5-13.

What is a Chapter 14-12 under AR 635-200 used for?

Acts or Patterns of Misconduct.

Field Sanitation

....

ATP 4-25.12, TC 4-02.3, TC 21-3, TC 3-21.75

What TC covers field hygiene and sanitation?

TC 4-02.3.

What ATP covers Unit Field Sanitation Teams?

ATP 4-25.12.

Where should the water point be located in the bivouac site?

Upwind of the latrine and garbage areas.

What is the most effective practice a Soldier can perform to protect themselves from the spread of disease?

Washing or sanitizing their hands frequently.

How should clothing be worn in a cold-weather environment?

In loose layers.

How far should latrines be positioned from food operations?

At least 100 meters down wind.

What is potable water?

Safe drinking water.

What is non-potable water?

Water that is not safe to drink.

Name three improvised latrines.

Cat hole, straddle trench, mound, deep pit, and board hole.

Who is responsible for constructing and maintaining field waste disposal facilities?

Unit details.

Who makes up the unit field sanitation team?

1 NCO and 1 Enlisted Soldier.

Define preventative medicine measures.

Simple common-sense actions that Soldiers can perform to prevent illness and disease.

Where must handwashing devices be positioned?

Outside of latrines and in food service areas.

Historically what is the percentage of non-battle injuries related to disease?

80%.

What is the most important item of supply to a military force?

Water.

What is Blackwater?

Water containing human waste.

What is graywater?

Wastewater from non-latrine sources.

What are two of the five methods for disinfecting non-potable water?

Calcium hypochlorite, water purification tablets, iodine, boiling, chlorine.

Underwear should be changed at least twice a week. If it is not possible to wash underwear, what action should be taken?

Crumple it, shake it, and air it for at least two hours.

How many levels of heat categories are there?

Five.

How many iodine tabs are used to disinfect water in a canteen?

Two.

How far are burn pits located away from troop locations?

At least 450 feet.

If a toothbrush is not available what can be used as an alternative?

A clean piece of cloth or a chewed twig.

Fighting Positions

....

TC 3-21.75

What are the two types of fighting positions?

Deliberate and hasty.

Why does a fighting position have sloping floors?

It encourages grenades to roll into the grenade sumps.

Describe the dimensions of a two-man fighting position.

Two M4's in length; two helmets wide; and arm pit deep to the tallest person.

If available, what can be used for a hasty fighting position?

A crater that is 2-3 feet wide.

First Aid

TC 21-3, STP 21-1, TC 3-21.75, TC 3-27.76, TC 4-02.1

General First Aid Knowledge

What subject does TC 4-02.1 cover?

First Aid.

Define Combat Lifesaver.

Non-medical Soldiers selected by their unit commander for additional training beyond basic first aid procedures.

Who provides Enhanced First Aid?

Combat lifesavers.

What are the three stages of Tactical Combat Casualty Care (TC3)?

Care under fire, tactical field care, and tactical evacuation.

If you are under fire and unable to get to a casualty to administer treatment, what should you tell the casualty to do?

Play dead.

Should you attempt to provide first aid when your own life is in imminent danger?

No.

When coming upon a casualty what should you do?

Ask in a loud but calm voice: Are you okay? Gently shake the casualty on the shoulder.

What does CCP stand for?

Casualty Collection Point.

In first aid, what does BSI stand for?

Body Substance Isolation.

If a casualty is wearing body, armor how do you check their response to pain?

Pinch the nose or the earlobe and check for responsiveness using the "AVPU" method.

Define First Aid?

Urgent and immediate lifesaving and other measures which can be performed for casualties (or performed by the casualty himself) by nonmedical personnel when medical personnel are not immediately available.

What does CASEVAC mean?

Casualty Evacuation.

What does ABCDE stand for?

ABC's of first aid; Airway, Breathing, Circulation, Disability, Exposures.

What does IFAK stand for?

Improved First Aid Kit.

What is the DD Form 1380?

Tactical Combat Casualty Care Card.

Name the types of blood vessels within the body.

Arteries, arteriole, capillaries, venules, and veins.

What is the abbreviation "AVPU" used for in first aid?

It is a method to determine the level of consciousness. A=alert, V=responds to voice, P=responds to pain, and U=unresponsive.

What are the first three actions a Soldier should take when they come upon a casualty?

Check for breathing; check for bleeding; and check for shock.

Abdominal Wounds

What is the most important concern in the initial first aid for abdominal injuries?

Shock.

When working with an abdominal wound, you should not apply pressure to which areas?

The wound or exposed organs.

When transporting a casualty with an abdominal wound, how should they be positioned?

On their back, face up with knees flexed; if evacuation is delayed, check for shock every five minutes; seek medical aid; and record actions on the TCCC DD Form 1380.

When treating an abdominal wound, you should not attempt to___?

Replace protruding internal organs or remove protruding foreign objects.

Bleeding

How should you check a casualty for bleeding?

Reassess any tourniquets; perform blood sweep of extremities, neck; sweep hands from the casualty's neck upwards to the top of the head (note if there is blood or brain tissue on your hand); place hands behind casualty's shoulders and pass them downward behind the back, thighs, and legs.

Once bleeding is under control, what is the next action you should take?

Position the casualty to open an airway.

What are the three methods for controlling bleeding?

Direct pressure, pressure dressing, and tourniquet.

After applying a direct pressure bandage and no pulse is felt, what should you do?

Adjust the dressing to re-establish circulation.

Whose bandage should you use when applying a bandage?

Use the casualty's bandage.

When applying a Hemostatic dressing how long should direct pressure be applied?

At least 3 minutes.

When applying an emergency bandage, how high should the gauze extend above the wound?

1-2 inches.

Apply a Tourniquet

After applying the emergency bandage and bleeding continues, what action should you take?

Apply a CAT tourniquet.

In first aid what does CAT stand for?

Combat Application Tourniquet.

How tight should the CAT be on the limb?

It should be tight enough that three fingers cannot slide between the band and the limb.

How should a tourniquet be applied?

Two to three inches above the wound.

After applying a tourniquet what should be written on the casualty with a marker?

The letter "T" should be placed on the casualty and the time of application with a marker; typically, on the forehead.

Blister Agent – Treatment for

A casualty has burns (blisters) caused by a blister agent, what action should you take?

Do not try to decontaminate the skin where blisters are present; if blisters have not formed you can decontaminate the skin.

With regard to burns, if in a CRBN environment should a wound be uncovered?

No, it could cause additional harm.

Breathing

When checking breathing, why do you look at the chest?

You are looking for equal rise and fall of the chest.

What are the two methods for opening the airway?

Head tilt/chin lift method, and jaw thrust method.

What is the abdominal thrust used for?

Clearing a conscious casualty's airway obstruction.

You are opening an airway on a casualty who may have a spinal injury. You should you NOT use what method to open the airway?

Should NOT use the head tilt/chin lift method.

Name the three parts of the respiratory system?

Airway, rib cage, and lungs.

What is the first thing you should do before administering first aid to a choking victim?

Ask them if they are choking.

What are the two methods for clearing a choking hazard?

Abdominal thrust and chest thrust.

Name the 2 methods for rescue breathing?

Mouth to mouth and mouth to nose.

During rescue breathing an adult should receive how many breaths?

12 to 20.

During rescue breathing a child should receive how many breaths?

15 to 30.

Burns
You are evaluating a casualty with burns. There is clothing stuck to the wound. What should you do?

Leave the clothing in place, do not attempt to remove.

What are the four types of burns?

Thermal, electrical, chemical, and laser.

If a casualty is the victim of an electrical burn, what should you do first?

Ensure the power source causing the burn is turned off.

What should be done for liquid chemical burns?

Remove the liquid by flushing with water.

With regard to burns, how should dry chemical be removed from the skin?

By carefully brushing them off with a clean dry cloth. If large amounts of water are available flush the area; otherwise do not apply water.

How should burning white phosphorus burns be treated?

Smother with water, wet cloth, or wet mud; keep area covered with wet material.

A casualty has received a laser burn, what action should you take?

Move the casualty away from the source while avoiding eye contact with the beam source; if possible, wear laser eye protection.

A casualty has burns on the face and genital area how should you apply a dressing?

No dressing is applied to these areas.

In regard to burns, what is the danger of synthetic materials such as nylon?

They may melt and cause further injuries.

What is the most dangerous of all chemical burning substances in a first aid situation?

Alkali- due to the penetrating factor; usually found in ammonia; lye; potassium; magnesium; and lime.

What are the three typical types of chemicals that cause burns?

Alkali, Acid, and Irritants.

Carbon Monoxide Poisoning
What is the treatment for carbon monoxide poisoning?

Move the Soldier to open air, keep still and warm, if necessary, administer mouth to mouth and/or CPR, evacuate to nearest medical facility.

What are some of the symptoms of carbon monoxide poisoning?

Headache, dizziness, confusion, nausea, ringing in the ears.

Carry Methods - Manual

When should manual carries be used to move a casualty with a neck or spine injury?

Only in life threatening situations; otherwise the manual carries should not be used.

Name the types of manual first aid carry positions.

Fireman's carry, neck drag, cradle-drop drag, and litters.

What are two types of improvised litters?

Poncho and jacket improvised litters.

If a spinal injury is suspected, how should a sling be applied?

It should not be tied around the casualty's neck; it should be pinned to the casualty's clothing.

What piece of equipment may be used to assist in pulling a casualty from a vehicle if an upward movement is required?

Pistol belt or similar material.

When is a fireman's carry used in first aid encounters?

For unconscious or severely injured casualties.

When is a neck drag carry used in first aid encounters?

In combat for short distances.

When is a cradle-drop drag carry used in first aid encounters?

To move a casualty who cannot walk when being moved up or down stairs.

When should the litter carry be used in first aid encounters?

If materials are available, if the casualty must be moved a long distance, or if manual carries will cause further injury.

Cold Injuries
Name three cold-weather injuries?

Hypothermia, frostbite, frostnip, snow blindness.

Hypothermia
What is hypothermia?

It is defined as a body core temperature below 95 degrees Fahrenheit.

What are the signs and symptoms of hypothermia?

Vigorous shivering; shivering may decrease or cease as core temperature falls; conscious but usually apathetic or lethargic; confusion; sleepiness; slurred speech; shallow breathing; very slow respiration; weak pulse; low or unattainable blood pressure; change in behavior with or without poor control over body movements. Uncoordinated movements, shock, and coma may occur as body temp drops. Core temperature below 95 degrees Fahrenheit.

What are the first aid procedures for hypothermia?

Mild: warm body evenly without delay (provide a heat source), keep dry, protect from elements, warm liquids may be given only to a conscious casualty; be prepared to start CPR; seek medical attention immediately; severe hypothermia: quickly stabilize body temp, attempt to prevent further heat loss, handle gently, and evacuate to nearest medical treatment facility ASAP.

What is required to properly diagnose hypothermia?

A rectal core temperature must be taken.

Frostbite
What is frostbite?

The freezing of skin.

What is the color of frostbite skin?

First it turns red and then becomes pale gray or waxy white.

What are the signs and symptoms of frostbite?

Numbness in affected area; tingling, blistered, swollen, or tender areas; pale, yellowish, waxy looking skin (grayish in dark skinned Soldiers); frozen tissue that feels wooden to the touch; and significant pain after rewarming. Tingling, stinging, aching sensation, and cramping pain.

What are the first aid measures for frostbite?

Rewarming at room temperature or using body heat; loosen or remove constricting clothing and remove jewelry; move casualty to a sheltered area; protect affected area from further cold or trauma; once thawed the tissue may not be allowed to freeze again; avoid exposure to excessive heat; seek medical attention; and evacuate casualty.

What are the two classifications of frostbite?

Superficial and deep.

When should frostbite be thawed?

Only when the Soldier will be moved to an area in which the possibility of refreezing is no longer present.

What are the signs and symptoms of Chilblain?

Lesions are swollen, tender itchy and painful; skin becomes swollen red (or darkening on darker Soldiers) and hot to the touch with rewarming; itching and burning sensation may continue for several hours after exposure.

What is the treatment for chilblain?

Area usually responds to locally applied warming (body heat). Do NOT rub or massage area. Seek medical treatment.

What is another name for frost nip?

Chilblains.

Snow Blindness
What are the signs and symptoms of snow blindness?

Scratchy feeling in the eyes as if from sand or dirt; watery eyes; pain, possible as late as 5 hours later; reluctant or unable to open eyes.

What are the first aid procedures for snow blindness?

Cover eyes with dark cloth and evacuate to medical facility.

CPR
What is the ratio of breaths to chest compressions?

30 compressions/2 breaths 30:2.

When giving chest compressions how many should be given at one time?

30.

When giving chest compressions how deep show the compression go?

At least 2 inches with each compression.

How should chest compression be delivered?

Straight down on the casualty's breastbone.

How fast should chest compressions be done?

30 compressions at a rate of 100 per minute, in a smooth fashion.

When should you stop chest compressions?

When the casualty is revived, you are too exhausted to continue, you are relieved by a health care provider, the casualty is pronounced dead, a second rescuer states I know CPR and joins you in performing two rescuer CPR.

If you cannot use mouth to mouth, what method of rescue breathing should you use?

Mouth to nose.

Dehydration
What are the signs of dehydration?

Loss of appetite, headache, excessive sweating, weakness, faintness, dizziness, nausea, muscle cramps, skin is moist, pale, and clammy.

What is the treatment for dehydration?

Keep warm, loosen clothes, replace lost fluids, rest, and seek additional medical treatment.

Diarrhea

Name a treatment for diarrhea?

Drinking tea leaves with water, eating charcoal, or make a solution of ground chalk, charcoal, or dried bones and treated water. Take 2 tablespoons every 2 hours.

Eye Injury

When treating an eye laceration what should be avoided?

Never put pressure on the eye or remove anything from the eye surface.

If an eyelid is torn off, how should it be handled?

Wrap fragment in a separate moist dressing and evacuate with casualty.

How should an eye injury be protected?

Using the eye shield provided in the IFAK.

If the eye shield in the IFAK is not available, how can you shield the injured eye?

Using a paper cup or cardboard cone.

How is an uninjured eye covered?

With a dry dressing or eye patch.

Fractures

What is a closed fracture?

One in which the bone does not break the skin.

What is an open fracture?

One in which the bone pierces the skin.

What are the signs and symptoms associated with a fracture?

Deformity, tenderness, swelling, pain, inability to move the injured part, protruding bone, bleeding, and discolored skin at injury site.

What are open fractures subject to?

Contamination and infection.

Head and Skull Injuries

What are the first aid procedures for a head injury?

Maintain patient's airway using the jaw thrust maneuver; dress head wounds; control bleeding; treat for shock; seek medical aid; and monitor for convulsions or seizures.

When treating a head wound and brain tissue is present, it is important that you do not __?

Apply pressure to or try to replace the brain tissue.

What are the symptoms of a concussion?

Unconsciousness followed by confusion; temporary, short term loss of some or all brain functions; headache or seeing double; may or may not have a skull fracture.

What is a contusion?

An internal bruise or injury. It is more serious than a concussion.

Heat Categories

Heat Injuries
Name the types of heat injuries and heat related conditions?

Heat cramps, heat exhaustion, heatstroke, heat rash, and sunburn.

How much time does proper heat acclimatization require?

Three to five days, but full acclimatization can take up to two weeks.

What is heat exhaustion?

It is dehydration and loss of body salt.

Why are heat exhaustion and heat cramps considered "canaries in the coal mine"?

Because if not properly treated they could lead to heat stroke.

What are the symptoms of heat exhaustion?

Dizziness, weakness, and/or fainting. Skin is cool and moist to the touch, nauseated and/or headache.

What is the treatment for heat exhaustion?

Move to cool shaded area, loosen clothing, pour water on casualty and fan to increase cooling effect of evaporation, provide at least one quart of water to replace lost fluids, elevate legs, and seek medical attention.

What are the symptoms of heat stroke (sunstroke)?

No sweating, hot dry skin, may experience headache, dizziness, nausea, vomiting, rapid pulse and respiration, seizures, mental confusion, may suddenly collapse and lose consciousness.

What is the treatment for heat stroke (sunstroke)?

Move to cool shaded area, loosen clothing, remove outer clothing (if situation allows), immerse in cool water if cool bath is not available pour cool water on the head and body. Fan to increase cooling effect of evaporation, if conscious, slowly consume one quart of water.

What is the treatment for heat cramps?

Move to shade, loosen clothing, drink one quart of cool water slowly every hour, monitor, seek medical attention if cramps persist.

What are the signs of heat cramps?

Muscle cramps in the arms, legs, and/or stomach. Has pale and wet skin and is experiencing dizziness and extreme thirst.

Hyponatremia
Typically, how is hyponatremia induced in Soldiers?

By consuming too much water at one time.

What are the signs and symptoms of hyponatremia?

Mental status change; vomiting; history of consumption of large amounts of water; poor food intake; abdomen distended/ bloated; and large amounts of clear urine.

What are the first aid procedures for hyponatremia (Water Intoxication)?

Do not give water or fluids by IV; if awake, allow Soldier to consume salty foods or snacks; seek medical aid; and evacuate immediately.

Immersion Foot
What are the signs and symptoms of immersion foot?

Cold, numb feet that may progress to hot with shooting pains; slight sensory change for two to three days; swelling, readiness, and bleeding may become pale and blue; aches and increase pain sensitivity and infection; loss of sensation; sever edema and gangrene; and loss of tissue.

What are the first aid steps for immersion foot?

Remove wet or constrictive clothing; gently wash and dry affected extremities; elevate affected limbs and cover with layers of loose, warm, dry clothing; DO NOT pop blisters, apply lotion or creams, massage; expose to heat, permit Soldier to walk; seek medical attention; and evacuate.

Impalement
How should an impalement injury be stabilized?

By placing several layers of bulky dressings around the injury site so that the dressing surrounds the object.

When a protruding object is present in an abdominal wound, what should you do with it?

Stabilize it.

If a casualty has an impalement injury in the cheek in which both ends of the object can be seen; how should it be removed?

Remove the object in the direction it entered.

MEDEVAC & 9 Line

Name the 5 patients' precedence on line 3 of a 9-line MEDEVAC

A: Urgent, B: Urgent - Surg, C: Priority, D: Routine, E: Convenience.

When listing the order of patient's precedence on a 9-line MEDEVAC and there are more than 2 categories of precedence what must the radio operator do?

Insert the word BREAK between each category.

When conducting medical air evacuations with a UH 60 or similar type of aircraft, when should you approach the aircraft from the rear?

You should NEVER approach the aircraft from the rear; stay in full view of the aircraft crew members.

Nerve Agent – Treatment for

What is the treatment for mild nerve agent poisoning?

Self-aid-use the ATNAA auto-injector.

How long should the ATNAA nerve agent injector be held in place?

For at least 10 seconds.

How many ATNAA injectors can be used when administering buddy aid for nerve agent poisoning?

No more than three.

When administering buddy aid for nerve agent poisoning and you must give the casualty their injection of ATNAA, what else must be done?

You must administer the CANA.

When a casualty has mild nerve agent poisoning, should the convulsant antidote for nerve agent (CANA) be administered?

No, the CANA should not be administered.

Once a nerve agent injector has been used, what should you do with it?

Bend the needle against a hard surface and attach to the blouse pocket flap.

What are three signs and symptoms of severe nerve agent poisoning?

Strange or confused behavior; wheezing, difficulty breathing, coughing; severely pinpointed pupils; red eyes with tearing; vomiting; severe muscular twitching; involuntary urination and defecation.

What are the two categories of nerve agent poisoning?

Mild and severe.

What are three signs and symptoms of mild nerve agent poisoning?

Unexplained runny nose; unexplained sudden headache; sudden drooling; tightness in chest or difficulty breathing; difficulty seeing; localized sweating and muscular twitching in the area of contaminated skin, stomach cramps, and nausea.

When injecting the ATNAA antidote for nerve agent, you administer the injection to the upper outer quarter of the buttock. Why is this important?

Failing to inject in the proper location increases the chance you may hit a major nerve causing paralysis.

If you have mild nerve agent poisoning what action should you take?

Self-administer 1 ANTNNA injector.

After giving yourself an initial ATNAA injection for nerve agent, should you administer a second injection?

No, do not give a second injection. If you are able to walk without assistance and know who you are and where you are, you will not need a second injection. Seek out a buddy to evaluate your symptoms.

Open Chest Wound

Prior to applying the bandage to an open chest wound what should you have the casualty do?

Fully exhale.

After treating an open chest wound how should you position the casualty?

Place them in the sitting position or injured side down.

When treating an open chest wound, what type of material is placed between the wound and the dressing?

Apply airtight material over the wound; you can use the casualty's outer wrapping for the field dressing.

When treating an open chest wound, how far should the material extend beyond the edge of wound?

At least two inches.

Shock

Name four symptoms of shock.

Sweaty but cool skin; pale skin, restlessness or nervousness; thirst; severe bleeding; confusion; rapid breathing; blotchy blue skin; nausea and/or vomiting.

What is the treatment for shock?

Move to shelter; shade from direct sunlight; lay casualty on back unless sitting allows for better breathing; elevate casualty's feet higher than the heart; loosen clothing; and prevent from getting chilled or overheated.

Flags, Guidons, Streamers, Tabards and Automobile Plates and Aircraft Plates

AR 840-10

What Regulation covers Flags, Guidons, Streamers, Tabards, and Automobile and Aircraft Plates?

AR 840-10.

How will an unserviceable flag be destroyed?

It will be destroyed privately and preferably by burning, shredding, or by some other method that does not show irreverence or disrespect to the flag.

When is the US flag displayed?

Daily from reveille to retreat.

In what position will the US flag always be carried?

In the position of honor; the marching right; or if there is a line of flags, it will be positioned in the center.

What is the proper method for raising the US flag to the Half-Staff Position?

It is first hoisted to the top of the pole then lowered to the half-staff position; When taken down, the flag will be raised to the top of the pole and then lowered for the day.

When can the US flag be flown upside down?

In times of distress.

How many streamers are attached to the US flag?

189 campaign streamers.

What is a Tabard?

A rayon banner of cloth for attachment to the tubing of a herald trumpet.

When an automobile plate is in place for a senior official and that official is not occupying the vehicle what action must be taken?

The plate will be covered or removed.

Guard Duty

TC 3-22.6

What subject does TC 3-22.6 cover?

Guard Duty.

What is your first general order?

I will guard everything within the limits of my post and quit my post only when properly relieved.

What is your second general order?

I will obey my special orders and perform all my duties in a military manner.

What is your third general order?

I will report violations of my special orders, emergencies, and anything not covered in my instruction, to the Commander of the Relief.

What are your special orders based on?

The current situation as well as the sensitivity of the site being protected.

Define interior guard.

Detailed by commanders of military installations to protect property and enforce specific military regulations.

Define exterior guard.

Used to classify those guards outside of a military installation, guards in a combat area, or hostile area.

If a guard observes any suspicious individual or individuals involved in a disturbance occurring on or near their post, what action should they take?

Apprehend using only the force necessary.

Who is required to respect a member of the guard force on duty?

All individuals regardless of rank.

Who are the only individuals authorized to give a guard orders or instructions?

Commanding Officer, Field Officer of the Day, Officers and NCOs of the Guard.

Does a guard on a post that requires a challenge salute?

No.

If a member of the military service finds an irresponsible guard on post, what must they do?

Notify the commander of the guard or an NCO of the guard and stay on the post until a qualified guard is posted.

When does a guard surrender their weapon?

Only when ordered to do so by the guard chain of command.

Anytime a guard is in doubt as to what action to take, what should they do?

Call the commander of the relief for instructions or assistance.

What is the primary responsibility of exterior guards?

Protect a unit from surprise and give the unit time to prepare to counter any threat.

What is the purpose of a guard mount?

To ensure all personnel are present, alert, properly equipped, knowledgeable, and capable of assuming duty.

What is the punishment for any person that discloses a countersign or patrol word?

Any person, in time of war, who discloses the parole word or countersign to any person not entitled to receive it, shall be punished by death or such other punishment as a court-martial deems appropriate.

If a group of individuals approach a guard post, how many are allowed to approach the position at one time?

Only one member of the group will approach for identification.

If a guard is not satisfied beyond a reasonable doubt that the individuals at their post are who they say they are, what action should the guard take?

Call the commander of the relief.

Who is responsible for ensuring guards are relieved from duty on time?

The commander of the guard.

Who is responsible for ensuring that all guard's reliefs are posted on time?

Sergeant of the Guard.

Who conducts guard mount?

Guard mounting is always conducted by the CoG or the SoG if the Commander is absent.

If a guard calls in for assistance who responses?

The Commander of the Relief.

When are Special Guards used?

When it is impractical to use members of the main guard to guard property or an area.

History

....

ADP 1-0, TC 7.21.13

What is the Army's history reflected in?

The battle and campaign streamers that adorn the Army flag.

What year was the Army established?

1775.

When was the Army flag dedicated?

14 June 1956.

Who was the first Commander in Chief of the Army?

George Washington.

When was the Declaration of Independence approved by Congress?

4 July 1776.

What was the name of the book Von Steuben wrote for order and discipline of the Army?

Regulations for the Order and Discipline of the Troops of the United States.

What Wording or Motto appears on the Army seal?

This We Will Defend.

When was the Creed of the Noncommissioned Officer written?

1973.

In the history of the wars the United States fought, which had the highest death toll?

Civil War.

What is the longest war in the history of the United States?

Afghanistan.

When does the Army celebrate its birthday?

14 June.

Who led the bombing raid over Tokyo in 1942?

Colonel James Doolittle.

Who is the most decorated Soldier of World War II?

Audie Murphy.

Where was the first atomic bomb dropped?

Hiroshima 1945.

When did World War I end?

11 November 1918.

What was the designated time for cessation of hostilities ending World War I?

The 11th month, on the 11th day, at the 11th hour.

What were the names of the beaches the allied forces landed on during World War II?

Omaha, Utah, Sword, Juno, Gold.

What started the Korean war?

North Korea's Invasion of South Korea.

Where did MacArthur conduct his famous amphibious assault of the Korean war?

Inchon.

What is the name of the Army Song?

The Army Goes Rolling Along.

In what war did America field the largest Army in American history?

World War II.

In what battle was George Custer killed?

Battle of Little Big Horn.

What Revolutionary War medal was reintroduced in 1932?

The Purple Heart.

On what date did terrorist fly planes into the World Trade Center?

11 September 2001.

On what date did the Japanese bomb Pearl Harbor?

7 December 1941.

What major North Vietnamese offensive took place in 1968?

The Tet Offensive.

What Sergeant Major of the Army was court-martialed and reduced in rank for numerous charges including sexual harassment?

SMA Gene McKinney.

What do the colors of the Army flag represent?

Red- hardiness and valor; White- purity and innocence; Blue-vigilance, perseverance, and justice.

Why is the color Blue especially significant to the Army?

Blue is the unofficial color of the Army for more than 200 years.

Land Navigation

....

TC 3-25.26, TC 21-3, STP 21-1

How do you convert kilometers to miles?

By multiplying the kilometers by .6. Example 80 km x .6= approximately 48 mph.

How do you convert miles to kilometers?

By multiplying miles by kilometers. Example 10 mph x 1.6 = 16 kph.

What manual covers Land Navigation and Map Reading?

TC 3-25.26.

What does TC 3-25-.26 cover?

Map Reading and Land Navigation.

How many degrees are in a circle?

360.

Define back azimuth.

The opposite direction of an azimuth. It is comparable to doing an about-face.

What is the back azimuth of 360?

180.

What are the 2 types of compasses?

Lensatic and M2 Artillery Compass.

One-click of the bezel ring on the lensatic compass is equal to how many degrees?

3 degrees.

What are the two ways to hold a compass?

Center hold, and Compass to Cheek.

Name three field expedient methods of land navigation?

Shadow tip, watch, and stars.

What star is used in the northern hemisphere for direction?

North Star.

What star is used in the southern hemisphere for direction?

Southern Cross.

What are the basic colors of a map?

Black, Red Brown, Blue, Green, Brown, Red.

What does the color BLACK represent on a map?

Manmade features.

What does the color RED BROWN represent on a map?

Contour lines, all relief features on a Red-Light Readable Map.

What does the color BLUE represent on a map?

Water.

What does the color GREEN represent on a map?

Vegetation.

What does the color BROWN represent on a map?

Relief Features and elevation.

What does the color RED represent on a map?

Cultural Features Populated areas and Main Roads.

How do you read coordinates on a map?

Right and up.

How close will a four-digit grid coordinate bring you to your target?

1000 meters.

How close will a six-digit grid coordinate bring you to your target?

100 meters.

How close does an eight-digit grid coordinate bring you to your target?

10 meters.

What is a pace count?

The number of steps it takes for a Soldier to walk 100 meters.

A pace or step is equal to how many inches?

30 inches.

What is the definition of a map?

A map is a graphic representation of a portion of the earth's surface drawn to scale as seen from above.

What are the five major terrain features?

Hill, Saddle, Valley, Ridge, and Depression.

What are the three minor terrain features?

Draw, Spur, Cliff.

What is the first step in reading a map?

Orient the map.

What is the back azimuth of 90 degrees?

270.

Define grid north.

Grid North is the top of any map established by using the vertical grid lines on the map usually symbolized by the letters GN.

Define Intersection.

Locating an unknown point by successively occupying at least 2 (preferably 3) known positions on the ground. Then map sighting the unknown location.

Define Resection.

A method of locating your position on a map by determining the grid azimuth to at least 2 (preferably 3) well-defined locations that can be pinpointed on a map.

How do you find the North Star?

Find the big dipper, the 2 stars at the end of the cup point to the North Star.

What are the three types of contour lines on a map?

Index, intermediate, and supplementary

What are three bar scales used on a military map?

Kilometers, Statute miles, and Nautical miles.

What is the formula for determining how long it will take to move from point A to point B?

T=D/R.

How do you determine direction using the shadow method in a northern area where the compass is unreliable?

In the northern hemisphere, shadows fall to the north side of objects; in the southern hemisphere, shadows fall to the south side of objects.

How many mils are in a circle?

6400.

How many mils are in 1 degree?

17.78 mils per degree.

What is the declination diagram?

The angular difference between 2 Norths.

What azimuth is used during resection when transferring the information to your map?

Back Azimuth.

What are the three steps in making a map overlay?

Orienting the overlay material, plotting and symbolizing the detail, and adding the required marginal information.

When using a compass and you need to bypass an obstacle and stay oriented what action should you take?

Steer around the obstacle using 90-degree increments until you have negotiated the obstacle and returned to your correct azimuth.

When using the shadow tip method to determine direction the first shadow always indicates which direction?

West.

Law of Land Warfare

FM 6-27, TC 3-21.75

What Manuals covers the law of land warfare?

FM 6-27, TC 3-21-.75.

If there is doubt as to the combatant status of a person how should their status as a POW be handled?

They will be treated as a POW pending determination of their status by a competent tribunal.

What are the two sources for the law of armed conflict?

Treaties and customary international law.

Describe a flag of truce.

A white flag.

What does a flag of truce indicate?

It only indicates a desire to communicate with the enemy and has no other significance.

What is the primary purpose of the law of land warfare?

1. Protect combatants, non-combatants, and civilians from unnecessary suffering. 2. Prevent degeneration of warfare into savagery and brutality.

What does the acronym LOAC stand for?

Law of Armed Conflict.

If a U.S. Soldier is captured (not in a POW status), wearing the uniform of our enemy how may they be treated?

As a spy.

Who has the right to status as a prisoner of war?

Any lawful combatant.

When can a US Soldier wear the uniform of an enemy and not be treated as a spy?

When escaping as a POW to return to friendly lines but they must not engage in combat while in enemy uniform.

How can an unprivileged belligerent be punished?

By trial and punishment of a military tribunal.

What are the main purposes of the Law of Armed Conflict?

1. Protecting combatants, non-combatants, and civilians from unnecessary suffering; 2. Providing certain fundamental protections for persons who fall into the hands of the enemy, particularly prisoners of war, military wounded and sick, and civilians; 3. Facilitating the restoration of peace; 4. Assisting the commander in ensuring the disciplined, ethical, and effective use of military force; 5. Preserving the professionalism and humanity of combatants; and 6. Preventing the degeneration of warfare into savagery or brutality.

Name three persons or objects that are not military objectives and are protected from being made the object of an attack so long as those protections have not been forfeited.

1. Individual civilians and the civilian population as such; 2. Military medical personnel and chaplains (see Chapter 4 for rules governing these personnel); 3. Individuals who are hors de combat; 4. Civilian objects or other protected objects, that is, all objects that are not military objectives; 5. Medical units, transport, and equipment; and 6. Undefended villages, towns, and cities.

What action can be taken against individuals who parachute from an aircraft in distress?

No action can be taken. They cannot be made the object of an attack.

What action can be taken against persons parachuting into combat?

They may be attacked throughout their descent and upon landing.

What action is required when a flag of truce is displayed?

No action is required as the opposing force is not required to cease fire merely because a flag of truces has been displayed.

How must all detainees be treated?

They must be treated humanely and protected against cruel, inhuman, or degrading treatment or punishment.

What action will be taken for any serious injury or death of a POW?

There will be an official investigation to determine the cause of the injury or death.

Leadership & Counseling

*ADRP 6-22, ADP 6-22, TC 7-21.13, TC 7-22.7,
AR 600-100*

Authority

What are the two types of Authority?

Command and General Military Authority.

Where does Command authority come from?

Policy, procedures, and precedents.

Define General military authority.

Authority extended to all Soldiers to take action and act in the absence of a unit leader or other designated authority.

Define Command authority.

The authority a commander lawfully exercises over subordinates by virtue of rank or assignment.

Where do NCOs obtain their authority?

From the Secretary of the Army as outlined in Army regulations.

How is military authority exercised?

Promptly, fairly, courteously, and firmly.

Leaders may delegate any or all of their authority to their subordinates unless ___

Restricted by law, regulation or a superior. Leaders cannot delegate authority they do not have.

What is delegation of authority?

The passing on of certain aspects of a mission or task to the appropriate level capable of handling the task or mission. This authority may be further delegated if need be.

When can a leader NOT delegate authority to a subordinate?

Leaders cannot delegate authority they do not have.

Counseling
What does a good counseling do?

It informs the Soldier what they are doing well, what they are doing wrong, and how to improve on their weaknesses.

What leader activity is central to leader development?

Counseling.

How many types of developmental counseling are there?

Three.

What are the three types of developmental counseling?

Event Counseling; Performance Counseling; Professional Growth Counseling.

Define Event Counseling.

Involves a specific event or situation.

What are some examples of event counseling?

Superior or substandard performance; Reception and Integration; Crisis; Referral; Promotion; Separation.

Define Performance Counseling.

When leaders conduct a review of a subordinate's duty performance over a certain period of time.

What does a performance counseling include?

Discussion of established performance objectives and standards for the next period; periodic performance counseling as a part of the NCOER support form requirements; beginning of and during the evaluation period and provides opportunity for leaders to establish and clarify expected values, attributes, and competencies.

Define Professional Growth Counseling.

A discussion designed to further the growth of an individual in their career.

What does a professional growth counseling include?

Planning for accomplishment of individual and professional goals; identify and discuss subordinate's strengths and weaknesses; create an individual development plan that builds on those strengths and weaknesses; opportunities for civilian and military schooling, future assignments, special programs, and reenlistment options.

Why do leaders counsel?

To let Soldiers, know what it takes to be successful today and tomorrow.

What are the four stages of the developmental counseling process?

Identify the need for counseling; prepare for counseling; conduct the counseling session; and follow-up.

Name the types of counseling.

Event; Reception and Integration; Crisis; Referral; Promotion; Transition; Adverse Separation; Performance; and Professional Growth.

What leader development process is defined as: a standardized process used to provide feedback to a subordinate?

Counseling.

What is one of the most important leadership development responsibilities of an Army?

Counseling.

What do the three Army leader development tools/multipliers (Counseling, Coaching, Mentoring) enhance and influence within the Army leader development model?

Maturity, shared identity, self-awareness, adaptability, conceptual and team building skills in all leaders.

Duties
What are the three types of duties an NCO has?

Specified duties; directed duties; and implied duties.

Define Specified duties.

Those related to jobs and positions (MOS related duties, Army Regulations, etc.).

Define Directed duties.

Those issued by superiors orally or in writing (CQ, Staff Duty, Key Control NCO, etc.).

Define Implied duties.

Often support specified duties but in some cases may not be related to MOS positions. May not be written but implied instructions. Duties usually depend on individual initiative (improve quality of life; keeps unit functioning at optimum level).

Leadership
What subject does TC 7-22.7 cover?

The Noncommissioned Officer Guide.

As a leader, what are your roles?

Trainer, disciplinarian, coach, and leader.

Define Leadership.

The process of influencing people by providing purpose, direction, and motivation to accomplish the mission and improve the organization.

What subject does ADRP 6-22 cover?

Army Leadership.

What ADRP covers Army Leadership?

ADRP 6-22.

What does the acronym LDRSHIP mean?

It represents the Army Values: Loyalty, Duty, Respect, Selfless Service, Honor, Integrity, and Personal Courage.

Define Discipline.

The glue that holds units together in order to accomplish the assigned mission and it is the culmination of the genuine acceptance of Army Values.

What is an important form of two-way communication to reach shared understanding?

Active listening.

What are the three developmental domains that shape the critical learning experiences throughout Soldiers' careers?

Institutional, Operational, Self-development.

Define "Toxic Leadership".

A combination of self-centered attitudes, motivations, and behaviors having an adverse effect on subordinates, the organization, and mission performance.

Name three of the five Destructive Leadership styles.

Incompetent managers; affable non-participant; insensitive; toxic self-centered abuser; and criminal.

Define the NCO Support Channel.

It parallels and complements the chain of command. It is a channel of communication and supervision from the CSM to the 1SG and then to other NCOs and enlisted personnel in the unit.

Who has the greatest impact on Soldiers?

First line leaders.

Mentoring & Coaching
What is Coaching?

A development technique used for a skill, task, or specific behavior.

Define Mentorship.

The voluntary developmental relationship that exists between a person of greater experience and a person of lesser experience that is characterized by mutual trust and respect.

What tools do Army leaders use to facilitate development of their subordinates in accordance with AR 600-100?

Counseling, Coaching, and Mentoring.

What leader development process is defined as: guiding another person's development in new or existing skills during the practice of those skills?

Coaching.

What leader development process is defined as: a voluntary development relationship that exists between a person of greater experience and a person of lesser experience, characterized by mutual trust and respect?

Mentoring.

Who relies primarily on teaching and guiding to help bring out and enhance current capabilities of an individual?

A coach.

A ___ helps people understand and appreciate their current level of performance and their potential, and instructs them on how to reach the next level of knowledge and skill.

Coach.

____ extends beyond the scope of chain of command and occurs when advice and counsel are provided.

Mentoring.

Effective mentoring has a positive effect on what aspects of a person's life?

Their personal and professional development.

Responsibility
Which one of the 14 NCO responsibilities do you believe are most important to you and why?

What are the most important responsibilities for an NCO?

Mission accomplishment and the welfare of their Soldiers.

What is Individual Responsibility?

Requirement to perform your duties to the best of your ability; personal conduct, & appearance; physical fitness, etc.

Define Rank Responsibility.

Those responsibilities based on rank, duty position, and even geographical location.

Define Accountability.

The requirement to answer to superiors for mission accomplishment. The obligation to answer for properly using delegated authority. Leaders are accountable for what they do.

Name the Army Values.

Loyalty, Duty, Respect, Selfless-Service, Honor, Integrity, and Personal Courage.

Define Loyalty.

Bear true faith and allegiance to the US Constitution, the Army, your unit, and other Soldiers.

Define Duty.

Fulfill your obligations.

Define Respect.

Treat people as they should be treated.

Define Selfless Service.

Put the welfare of the Nation, the Army, and your subordinates before your own.

Define Honor.

Live up to Army Values.

Define Integrity.

Do what is right, legally and morally.

Define Personal Courage.

Face fear, danger, or adversity (physical and moral).

Leaves and Passes

AR 600-8-10

What regulation covers Leaves and Passes?

AR 600-8-10.

What action will be taken if a Soldier has a leave balance of 60 days and waits until late in the year to take leave?

The Soldier will be informed that they risk loss of leave if the operational situation requires their presence.

How many days of leave are accrued each month?

2.5 days per month.

What is convalescent leave?

Nonchargeable absence from duty granted to expedite a Soldier's return to full duty after illness, injury, or childbirth.

A regular pass will not exceed how many days?

Will not exceed three days in length to include public holiday weekends or public holiday periods specifically extended by the President.

What are the two types of Special Passes?

Three and four day.

How much emergency leave can be granted for immediate family or loco parentis?

Up to 30 days.

From what location must a Soldier begin and end a regular pass?

It beings or ends on post, at a duty location, or at the location from where the Soldier normally commutes to duty; the Soldier must be physically at one of these locations when departing or returning from a regular pass.

What is the length of a three day regular pass?

A three-day pass period which includes a national holiday, begins at the end of the normal duty day on a Friday afternoon and terminates at the beginning of the normal duty day on the 4th day (Tuesday).

What is the rule when granting back to back passes?

Passes may not be granted back to back without a duty day in between the absences.

What must a Special Pass include with regard to days of the week?

If must include at least two duty days.

How may a Soldier request a leave extension?

In person; by telephone; message; or other convenient means through appropriate overseas commander, military installation, or activity nearest the leave address; or the Red Cross.

Military Justice

AR 27-10

What regulation covers Military Justice?

AR 27-10.

When is the use of nonjudicial punishment appropriate?

In all cases involving minor offenses in which non-punitive measures are considered inadequate or inappropriate.

What are non-punitive measures?

Those actions taken by leaders to correct minor infractions that do not rise to the level nonjudicial punishment. For example: A Soldier would be given corrective training as a non-punitive measure to correct substandard performance.

What is nonjudicial punishment?

Punishment for minor offenses that cannot be addressed using the lesser measures of non-punitive measures. For example: A Soldier would receive an Article 15 for an offense because corrective training is not sufficient to address the violation.

What is the purpose of nonjudicial punishment?

Correct; educate; reform offenders whom the imposing commander determines cannot benefit from less stringent measures; preserve a Soldier's record of service from unnecessary stigma by record of court-martial conviction; further efficiency by disposing of minor offenses in a manner requiring less time and personnel than trial by court-martial.

What type of conduct do non-punitive measures usually deal with?

Misconduct resulting from: simple neglect, forgetfulness, laziness, inattention to instructions, sloppy habits, immaturity, difficulty adjusting to military life and similar deficiencies.

Do non-punitive measures constitute punishment? Explain.

No; non-punitive measures do not constitute punishment. They are tools for teaching proper standards of conduct and performance.

Why is nonjudicial punishment imposed?

To correct misconduct in violation of the UCMJ. This conduct usually results from intentional disregard of or failure to comply with prescribed standards of military conduct.

Give three examples of non-punitive measures.

Denial of pass or other privileges, counseling, administrative reduction in grade, administrative reprimands and admonitions, extra training, bar to reenlistment, and MOS reclassification.

What are the rules pertaining to extra training, extra instruction, corrective training?

Must relate directly to the offense; must be oriented to correct the deficiency; may be conducted after normal duty hours, cannot be punishment or perceived as punishment, will be discontinued once the deficiency is corrected.

What is the maximum punishment that may be imposed under the summary proceeding of an Article 15?

14 days extra duty; restriction for 14 days; oral reprimand or admonition; any combination of these actions.

How long does a Soldier have to submit an appeal when receiving a Summary Article 15?

Normally five calendar days.

Under the formal proceedings of an Article 15, how long does a Soldier have to decide if they will demand trial by court martial? Are they allowed to seek legal counsel during duty hours?

A Soldier will normally be given 48 hours to seek legal counsel and determine if they want trial by court-martial; they will also be allowed time off from duty to seek legal counsel.

What is the maximum punishment that can be imposed during a company grade Article 15?

Admonition/Reprimand: 14 days extra duty; 14 days restriction; 7 days correctional custody; 3 days diet confinement (on board a vessel for E-1 thru E-3); reduction in grade by 1 grade for E-1 thru E-4; forfeiture of 7 days' pay.

What is the maximum punishment that can be imposed during a field grade Article 15?

Admonition/Reprimand: 45 days extra duty; 60 days restriction; 30 days correctional custody; 4 days diet confinement (on board a vessel for E-1 thru E-3); reduction in grade by 1 or more grades (E-1 thru E-4), reduction of 1 grade for NCO during peace time; forfeiture of 1/2 months' pay for 2 months.

How long can punishment be suspended for company and field grade Article 15s?

No more than six months.

How long can punishment be suspended for a Summarized Article 15?

No more than three months.

If an appeal is not made in a timely manner, what action may be taken by the appeal authority?

The appeal may be rejected as untimely and no action will be taken.

What is the purpose of an Article 138 complaint?

It is a formal complaint filed against a commanding officer.

What action must a Soldier take before submitting an Article 138 complaint?

The Soldier must first attempt to solve the issue by submitting a written and signed Initial Request for Redress. In addition, an electronic message will also satisfy this requirement.

How long does a commander have to respond to a Soldier's Initial Request for Redress?

The response must be within 15 days. It must be written; an electronic message will satisfy this requirement.

How long does a Soldier have to submit an Article 138 complaint from the time of the wrong?

90 days from the discovery of the wrong.

Who ultimately receives the Article 138 for action?

The General Court-Martial Convening Authority.

A Soldier is being considered for an Article 15 for disrespect to an Officer. While the paperwork is being processed for the Article 15, the Soldier is found to have lied to an NCO in the performance of their duties. The command recommends the Soldier for a second Article 15. Is this legal? Explain.

It is not legal. When the Soldier is being considered for punishment under Article 15 all incidents at the time will be disposed of under one Article 15 proceeding.

What is the statute of limitation for the imposition of punishment under the proceeding of an Article 15?

Nonjudicial punishment may not be imposed for any offense that was committed more than two years before the date of imposition.

What unique punishment can be imposed on a Soldier embarked or attached to vessel?

Confinement on bread and water or diminished rations for a PFC or below.

Define remission.

An action in which any portion of the unexecuted punishment is canceled.

There are restrictions as to what extra duty cannot include. What are the restrictions?

Extra duty cannot be: cruel or unusual punishment; using the offender as a personal servant; duty normally intended as an honor; the offender cannot be required to perform a task that is ridiculous or degrading (example: cleaning a barracks floor with a toothbrush); any task that is a safety or health hazard; any task that would demean the Soldier's position as an NCO or specialist.

Define mitigation.

The reduction in either the quantity or quality of a punishment. Example: a punishment of correctional custody for 20 days is reduced to 10 days or to restriction for 20 days.

Movement - Tactical

....

TC 3-21.75

With regard to tactical movement techniques, when should a Soldier use the low crawl?

When crossing places where the cover and/or concealment are very low and enemy fire or observation prevents the Soldier from getting into a higher position as in high crawl or standing.

With regard to tactical movement techniques, what is the advantage of using the high crawl?

Allows you to move faster than the low crawl and still gives the Soldier visibility while still maintaining a low silhouette.

With regard to tactical movement techniques, when using the "RUSH" technique of movement, how long should you be exposed?

Three to five seconds.

With regard to tactical movement techniques, an aerial flare appears, what should you do to protect your night vision?

Close one eye while the flare is burning.

With regard to tactical movement techniques, name three tactical movement techniques?

Traveling, traveling overwatch, and bounding overwatch.

With regard to tactical movement techniques, when crossing any trails, what two key elements should you look for in a crossing spot?

Cover and concealment.

NCO Support Channel

....

AR 600-20, TC 7-21.13

Define the NCO support channel.

It parallels and complements the chain of command. It is a channel of communication and supervision from the CSM to the 1SG and then to other NCOs and enlisted personnel of the unit.

When is an NCO or enlisted Soldier allowed or required to assume command of a unit?

In the absence or disability of all officers in the unit. Pending the assignment and arrival of the new commander, the enlisted person will exercise temporary command of the unit.

Name the Sergeant Major of the Army

Name the Corps CSM

Name your Division CSM

Name your Brigade CSM

Name your Battalion CSM

Name your First Sergeant

Name your Squad/Section Leader

Name Your Team Leader

Oaths, Creeds, Army Song

Recite the Soldier's Creed and the Warrior Ethos.

I am an American Soldier. I am a warrior and a member of a team. I serve the people of the United States and live the Army values. I will always place the mission first. I will never accept defeat. I will never quit. I will never leave a fallen comrade. I am disciplined, physically and mentally tough, trained and proficient in my warrior tasks and drills. I always maintain my arms, my equipment, and myself. I am an expert and I am a professional. I stand ready to deploy, engage, and destroy the enemies of the United States of America in close combat. I am a guardian of freedom and the American way of life. I am an American Soldier.

Recite the Army Song.

Verse:

March along, sing our song, with the Army of the free. Count the brave, count the true, who have fought to victory. We're the Army and proud of our name! We're the Army and proudly proclaim:

First Chorus:

First to fight for the right, And to build the Nation's might, And the Army goes rolling along. Proud of all we have done, Fighting till the battle's won, And the Army goes rolling along.

Refrain:

Then it's hi! hi! hey! The Army's on its way. Count off the cadence loud and strong; For where'er we go, You will always know That the Army goes rolling along.

Second Chorus:

Valley Forge, Custer's ranks, San Juan Hill and Patton's tanks, And the Army went rolling along. Minute men, from the start, Always fighting from the heart, And the Army keeps rolling along.

Refrain:

Then it's hi! hi! hey! The Army's on its way. Count off the cadence loud and strong; For where'er we go, You will always know That the Army goes rolling along.

Third Chorus:

(slower, more freely)

Men in rags, men who froze, Still that Army met its foes, And the Army went rolling along. Faith in God, then we're right, And we'll fight with all our might, As the Army keeps rolling along.

Refrain:

Then it's hi! hi! hey!

The Army's on its way.

Count off the cadence loud and strong; (two! three!)

For where'er we go,

You will always know

That the Army goes rolling along! (keep it rolling!)

And the Army goes rolling along!

Recite the NCO Creed.

No one is more professional than I. I am a noncommissioned officer, a leader of Soldiers. As a noncommissioned officer, I realize that I am a member of a time-honored corps., which is known as the "The Backbone of the Army". I am product of the Corps of noncommissioned officers and will at all times conduct myself so as to bring credit upon the Corps, the military service and my country regardless of the situation in which I find myself. I will not use my grade or position to attain pleasure, profit, or personal safety. Competence is my watchword. My two basic responsibilities will always be uppermost in my mind; accomplishment of my mission and the welfare of my Soldiers. I will strive to remain technically and tactically proficient. I am aware of my role as a noncommissioned officer. I will fulfill my responsibilities inherent in that role. All Soldiers are entitled to outstanding leadership; I will provide that leadership. I know my Soldiers and I will always place their needs above my own. I will communicate consistently with my Soldiers and never leave them uninformed. I will be fair and impartial when recommending both rewards and punishment. Officers of my unit will have maximum time to accomplish their duties; they will not have to accomplish mine. I will earn their respect and confidence as well as that of my Soldiers. I will be loyal to those with whom I serve; seniors, peers, and subordinates alike. I will exercise initiative by taking appropriate action in the absence of orders. I will not compromise my integrity, nor my moral courage. I will not forget, nor will I allow my comrades to forget that we are professionals, noncommissioned officers, leaders!

Recite the NCO Charge.

I will discharge carefully and diligently the duties of the grade to which I have been promoted and uphold the traditions and standards of the Army. I understand that soldiers of lesser rank are required to obey my lawful orders. Accordingly, I accept responsibility for their actions. As a noncommissioned officer, I accept the charge to observe and follow the orders and directions given by supervisors acting according to the laws, articles and rules governing the discipline of the Army, I will correct conditions detrimental to the readiness thereof. In so doing, I will fulfill my greatest obligation as a leader and thereby confirm my status as a noncommissioned officer.

Operational Security (OPSEC)

AR 530-1

What regulation covers operations security?

AR 530-1.

Define Operational Security.

A process that identifies critical information of military plans and indicators that might reveal it, then develops measures to eliminate, reduce, or conceal these indicators.

What does OPSEC stand for?

Operational Security.

What can potentially result from failure to properly implement OPSEC?

Serious injury or death to personnel: damage to weapons systems, equipment, and facilities; loss of sensitive technologies; and Mission failure.

Who is the ultimate authority for implementing OPSEC?

The commander.

What type of information does OPSEC protect?

Critical information that is both classified and unclassified.

What is Physical Security?

Protective measures to deny unauthorized personnel access to specific area, facilities, material, or classified information.

What is COMSEC?

Communications Security.

What does HUMINT stand for?

Human Intelligence.

What does IMINT stand for?

Imagery Intelligence.

What does SIGINT stand for?

Signals Intelligence.

What does MASINT stand for?

Measurement and Signature Intelligence.

What does TECHINT stand for?

Technical Intelligence.

What does OSINT stand for?

Open Intelligence Source.

What does IA stand for?

Information Assurance.

What does SEDA stand for?

Subversion and Espionage Directed Against the Army.

Physical Fitness

FM 7-22, ATP 7-22.01, ATP 7-22.02

NOTE: The ACFT has not been fully implemented as of this printing. Therefore we provided information on the ACFT and APFT. The old FM 7-22 is used for answering APFT questions.

APFT

Please note as of this printing the final documentation for the AFCT has not been published. We have provided the most up to date information available. Please check our website for electronic updates to this section.

What Manual covers army physical readiness training?

FM 7-22

In what order must an APFT be performed?

Push-ups, sit-ups, and 2-mile run.

What are the commands for the extended rectangular formation?

Extend to the left March, arms downward move, left face, extend the left March, arms downward move, right face, count off, even numbers to the left uncovered.

What is the command to reassemble the extended rectangular formation?

Assemble to the right March.

Name four times when a Soldier should not be tested for the APFT?

1. When ill or fatigued
2. When they have participated in tiring duties
3. When weather or environmental conditions may inhibit physical performance
4. When it would violate a medical profile

How often must a Soldier take the APFT at a minimum?

At least once every six months.

Before taking an APFT, what must the commander specify?

If the test is for record.

The 2-mile run course should be free of what type of hazards?

Traffic, slippery surfaces, and heavy pollution.

What constitutes a repetitive APFT failure?

When a Soldier has been provided adequate time and assistance (not to exceed 90 days) and fails a retest.

What action is taken for Soldiers who fail a record APFT or fail to take a record APFT within 12 months?

The Soldiers will be flagged in accordance with AR 600-8-2.

How often may a commander minister the APFT?

As often as they wish; however, they must specify beforehand when the APFT is for record.

How will a Soldier be scored if they become ill during the APFT and cannot complete the test?

They are a test failure.

If a Soldier is profiled for two or more APFT events what does their APFT consist of?

Two mile run or an alternate aerobic event.

From start to finish the APFT must be completed within what time frame?

From start to finish the APFT can take no longer than two hours.

What are the requirements for the APFT running the course?

A flat, measured two mile running course with a solid surface with no more than a 3% grade.

When may a mat be used during the APFT?

During the push-up and sit up event as long as the entire body is on the mat.

How many days does a Soldier need post deployment before taking an APFT?

90 days.

How is the APFT two mile run course surveyed?

It is not surveyed but it must be measured.

What are the authorized alternate events for the APFT?

800 yard swim
6.2 miles stationary ergometer test
6.2 mile bicycle test
2.5 mile walk

How much rest is allowed between APFT events?

A minimum of 10 and a maximum of 20 minutes.

ACFT

Please note as of this printing the future of the ACFT is in question so we have prepared these questions from the doctrine that was released as of October 2020.

What manual governs the ACFT test?

ATP 7-22.01

What are the events for the ACFT?

(1) Three Repetition Maximum Deadlift; (2) Standing Power Throw; (3) Hand Release Push Up (HRP) - Arm Extension; (4) Sprint Drag Carry; (5) Leg Tuck (Alternate Plank); (6) Two Mile Run

How many events does the ACFT test consist of?

6

What does the ACFT validate?

The Soldier's and unit's physical readiness training.

What does the acronym H2F stand for?

Holistic Health and Fitness System.

What is the intent of the ACFT?

To accurately reflect the Soldier's combat performance capability linked to Warrior Tasks and Battle Drills (WTBD) and Common Soldier Tasks (CST).

The events of the ACFT help predict a Soldier's performance on what type of tasks?

Warrior Tasks and Battle Drills as well as Common Tasks.

The ACFT trains and tests the physical capabilities of the Soldier and it also assesses what other capability?

Mental toughness.

What does the ACFT assess with regard to fatigue?

It tests the Soldier's ability to move under fatigue, ability to concentrate, and keep going to sustain lethality.

How do commanders ensure Soldiers will perform well during the ACFT?

By ensuring Soldiers are not tested when fatigued, ill or on temporary profile for a physical condition and ensuring Soldiers do not participate in fatiguing duties before taking the test.

Since the ACFT can be resource intensive explain the self-administrated ACFT process?

There is no self-administration of the ACFT. Soldiers are not authorized to self-administer the ACFT for record test purposes.

How many Soldiers are required to administer the ACFT to one Soldier?

3.

Name the three individual positions required to administer the ACFT to a Soldier?

OIC or NCOIC and 2 Graders.

How many graders are required for the ACFT?

2.

For timed ACFT events how many stopwatches are required?

Two, a primary and a backup.

How many minutes does the Soldier have for the LEG Tuck?

Two minutes.

A 16 lane ACFT test site provides the capacity to test how many Soldiers in 120 minutes or less?

64.

How large does the test area for the ACFT have to be?

30 meters by 50 meters.

What are the requirements for a test site?

An area measuring 30m x 50m on grass or artificial turf, free of any significant hazards, an area to conduct preparation drill and recovery drill, a soft flat area for field-based events.

What are the course requirements for the 2 Mile Run event?

Generally flat, measured running course with a solid, improved surface with no more than 3 percent uphill grade and has no overall decline. The start and finish must be at the same altitude.

The 2 Mile Run course should be free of what type of hazards?

(1) Traffic, (2) Slippery road surfaces, (3) Heavy air pollution

What are the minimum and maximum weight requirements for three Repetition Maximum Deadlift?

140 lbs. and 340 lbs. respectively

What are the time restrictions for conducting the ACFT?

The events must be completed in order on the same day during a test period not to exceed 120 minutes to include the preparation drill and Maximum Deadlift preparation.

What is the definition of the ACFT test period?

The period of time that elapses from the start of the preparation drill to the finish of the 2 Mile Run.

How much rest is given after the Leg Tuck and when does it start?

10 minutes, it starts when the last Soldier completes the Leg Tuck.

What is the maximum number of Soldier that will rotate through a lane at any one time?

4.

How much rest is given between ACFT events?

Other than the 10-minute rest after the last Soldier completes the Leg Tuck there are no programmed rests between events nor a required amount of rest per Soldier.

How many restarts are allowed during the ACFT?

There are no restarts.

When must questions concerning grading or other issues regarding the ACFT be resolved?

All questions must be resolved by the OIC or NCOIC within the 120-minute time limit.

How is a video recording used during the ACFT?

It can be used for training purposes but it will not be used to adjudicate event scores.

What items are not authorized for wear during the ACFT?

(1) Any piece of clothing not part of the APFU; (2) Devices or equipment that offer any potential for unfair advantage; (3) Nasal strips; (4) Back braces; (5) Elastic bandages; (6) Limb braces

What electronic devices are eligible for wear during the ACFT?

(1) Biometric measuring devices such as watches; (2) Heart rate monitors; (3) Step counter and fitness trackers are permitted; (4) No other electronic devices are permitted

Which Soldier will go first during the Standing Power Throw?

The Soldier who achieved the lowest weight on the Maximum Deadlift. The order remains the same for the next four events.

What is the order of events for the ACFT?

(1) Three Maximum Deadlift; (2) Standing Power Throw;
(3) Hand Release Pushups; (4) Sprint Drag Carry;
(5) Leg Tuck (Alternate Plank); (6) Two-Mile Run

What do graders issue each Soldier for the 2 Mile Run?

Graders will issue each Soldier a vest or a number.

What does the Soldier's signature on the ACFT scorecard validate?

The Soldier's signature means they concur with the score.

What is the minimum score for each ACFT event?

60 points in each event for a minimum passing score of 360 points.

What is the maximum score a Soldier can earn on the ACFT?

600 points.

During the three Maximum Deadlift if a Soldier fails on the first attempt what action may they take?

They are allowed to attempt a lower weight.

Does a safety stop during the first repetition of the MDL count for record?

No.

Give three examples when the MDL attempt be terminated.

If during any of the three repetitions the Soldier:
(1) Drops the bar to the ground; (2) Removes their hands from the bar between repetitions when the bar is on the ground; (3) Fails to touch the bar to the ground between repetitions; (4) Does not perform a continuous movement by resting on the ground; (5) Is called for a safety stop on the 2nd or 3rd repetition of an attempt

How is the ball landing measurement taken for the Standing Power Throw?

Taken from the center of the ball's landing point perpendicular to the tape measure to the nearest decimeter.

Give three examples of when a repetition will not count during the Hand Release Pushup.

(1) Failing to maintain a straight body; (2)Failing to fully extend elbows in the up position; (3) Failing to bring the hands back to the staring position to complete the repetition; (4) Failing to keep the feet within a boot's width apart

Give three examples of when the Hand Release Pushup event will be terminated.

If the Soldier: (1) Deviates from the straight body alignment while in the Front lean and rest position; (2) Lifts a foot or hand from the ground; (3) Places a knee on the ground from the front lean and rest position; (4) Repeats the hand release movement before raising up from the ground; (5) Rests on the ground

What are the ACFT MOD Aerobic events?

5,000-meter row, 12,000-meter bike, 1,000-meter swim

How much time is allotted for the ACFT MOD Aerobic events?

25 minutes.

What does OPAT Stand for?

Occupational Physical Assessment Test.

What does ACFT stand for?

Army Combat Fitness Test.

What does CWST stand for?

Combat Water Survival Test.

Name three of five poor lifting habits.

(1) Rounding of the spine; (2) Knees collapsing in words;
(3) Failure to reach the standing position; (4) Failure to touch
the weights down on the ground; (5)Uncontrolled movement
or tilting of the hex bar

How is the ACFT Two-mile course surveyed?

There is no requirement to survey the course.

How many minutes does a Soldier have to complete the ACFT?

120 minutes.

When must a Soldier with a temporary profile take the six event ACFT?

After completing rehabilitation and reconditioning.

What subject does ATP 7-22.01 cover?

Holistic Health and Fitness Testing.

What manual covers Holistic Health and Fitness Testing?

ATP 7-22.01

What manual covers holistic health and fitness drills and exercises?

ATP 7-22.02

What subject does ATP 7-22. 02 cover?

Holistic health and fitness drills and exercises.

What manual covers pregnancy and postpartum physical training drills?

ATP 7-22.02

What manual should be used to develop a physical training program?

ATP 7-22.02

What commands are given to reassemble the formation from an extended rectangular formation?

Assemble to the right, March.

What are the commands to execute the extended rectangular formation?

(1) Extend the left, march; (2) Arms downward, move; (3) Left, face extend to the left, march; (4) Arms downward, move; (5) Right, face; (6) From front to rear, count off; (7) Even numbers to the left, uncover

What does the acronym P3T stand for?

Pregnancy and postpartum physical training

Where can videos on strength training circuits be found?

The Central Army Registry.

Name one of the two types of command use during physical training?

Preparatory commands and commands of execution.

Name two types of company formations during physical training.

(1) Company in line with platoons in column; (2) Company formation En Masse; (3) Platoon extended a rectangle formation covered

What FM covers holistic health and fitness?

FM 7-22

What subject does FM 7-22 cover?

Holistic health and fitness.

What manual covers the overarching program for the holistic health and fitness system?

Field Manual 7-22

What is the overarching goal of the holistic health and fitness system?

Soldier readiness.

What does the abbreviation BMI stand for?

Body mass index.

On average how much weight can a Soldier lose per week?

0.5–1 pound per week.

What is the only organ of the body that requires sleep?

The brain.

What manual covers the overarching program for the holistic health and fitness system?

Field Manual 7-22

What is the overarching physical training goal of the holistic health and fitness system?

Movement lethality—the ability to physically engage with and destroy the enemy.

To prevent lean muscle loss and nutrient deficiencies women should consume how many calories per day?

1200 cal per day.

To prevent lean muscle loss and nutrient deficiencies men should consume how many calories per day?

1500 cal per day.

One of the three basic interrelated principles of sleep health?

Sleep duration, Sleep timing, Sleep continuity

Promotions

TC 7-21.13, AR 600-8-19

What is the process for promotions?

Train, Select, Promote.

What regulation covers Enlisted Promotions and Reductions?

AR 600-8-19.

What does the acronym STEP mean?

Select, Train, Educate, Promote.

If a Soldier (PV2-SSG) is fully qualified for promotion but is not recommended for promotion, what action must the first line leader take?

Formally counsel the Soldier when the Soldier obtains full eligibility and every three months thereafter.

When counseling a fully eligible, not recommended Soldier, what must the counseling contain?

The counseling will include information as to why the Soldier was not recommended and what the Soldier must do to correct the deficiencies or qualities that reflect a lack of promotion potential.

What are the automatic promotion requirements for promotion to PV2?

6 months' time in service.

What are the automatic promotion requirements for promotion to PFC?

12 months' time in service; 4 months' time in grade.

What are the automatic promotion requirements for promotion to SPC?

24 months' time in service; six months' time in grade.

What can be waived for promotion to PV2?

TIS may be waived from six months to four months.

What can be waived for promotion to PFC?

TIS may be waived from 12 months to six months; TIG may be waived from four months to two months.

What can be waived for promotion to SPC?

TIS may be waived from 24 months to 18 months; TIG may be waived from six months to three months.

What does TIS stand for?

Time in Service.

What does TIG stand for?

Time in Grade.

What are the TIG and TIS requirements in the secondary zone for promotion to SGT?

17 months TIS / 5 months TIG.

What are the TIG and TIS requirements in the primary zone for promotion to SGT?

35 months TIS / 11 months TIG.

What are the TIG and TIS requirements in the secondary zone for promotion to SSG?

47 months TIS / 6 months TIG.

What are the TIG and TIS requirements in the Primary zone form promotion to SSG?

71 months TIS / 17 months TIG.

For promotion to SGT, what level of SSD must be completed prior to board appearance?

SSD/DLC 1.

For promotion to SSG, what level of SSD must be completed prior to board appearance?

SSD/DLC 2.

Must a promotion board at the E5/E6 level include a minority member?

Yes, if reasonably available.

When does the president of the promotion board vote?

To break a tie.

What is the minimum number of voting members a board must have?

3.

All voting members must be _____ to the Soldier being recommended for promotion.

Senior in Rank.

If an officer presides over a SGT/SSG board what is the minimum rank authorized?

Captain or CW3.

Are there any minority requirements for conducting an E5/E6 promotion board?

Yes, voting member of the board WILL include a minority. When this is not possible the promotion authority WILL provide the reason for the absence of a minority in the appointment memorandum.

Retention

....

AR 601-280, DA PAM 601-280, TC 7-21.13

Where can you find information on bars to continued service?

AR 601-280 chapter 8.

What is the correct terminology for a bar?

Bar to Continued Service.

Is a bar to reenlistment an administrative action or a punitive action?

Punitive.

Upon completion of each three-month review period for Soldiers fully eligible for promotion in the primary zone, who failed to complete the required SSD/DLC course, what action must the commander take?

Counsel the Soldier using the DA FORM 4856 to inform the Soldier that the bar has been reviewed, and will remain in effect unless the Soldier completes the mandatory SSD/DLC courses.

What regulation covers the Army retention program?

AR 601-280.

What action must a commander take if after the second three-month review period the bar is not recommended for removal?

The commander will initiate separation proceedings under AR 635-200.

What is the process for barring a Soldier if they refuse to reenlist?

Soldiers cannot be barred because they refuse to reenlist.

What is the purpose of the Army Retention Program?

Ensures only those Soldiers who have maintained a record of acceptable performance will be offered the privilege of reenlisting with the Active Army, or transferring to the Reserve Component.

What does QMP stand for?

Quality Management Program.

Safety

....

AR 385-10, DA PAM 385-10, TC 7-21.13, TC 7-22.7

What Army Regulation Covers the Army Safety Program?

AR 385-10.

At a minimum, how often will a Soldier's privately owned vehicle be inspected by the unit?

At least every six months.

What items will be checked during a unit inspection of a Soldier's privately owned vehicle?

Verification of driver's license, insurance, and registration; Unit inspectors will also follow local vehicle checklists.

Define Risk Management

The Army process for identifying, assessing, and controlling risks and then making decisions that balance risk cost with benefits.

If a Soldier's car fails a unit safety inspection, can a leader demand or order the Soldier to surrender their vehicle keys?

No; they can order the Soldier not to drive the vehicle but cannot take any personal property.

With regard to Safety, what does PPE stand for?

Personal, Protective, Equipment.

What Army Program has the biggest impact on Soldier Readiness?

The Army Safety Program.

Where can information on the Safety Awards program be found?

DA PAM 385-10.

Salutes, Honors, Customs, Courtesy

....

AR 600-25, TC 7-22.7, TC 3-21.75

What is the purpose of the NCO induction ceremony?

It is meant to celebrate the transition of a Soldier to a leader as they join the ranks of a professional NCO Corps.

What regulation covers Salutes, Honors, and Visits of Courtesy?

AR 600-25.

Who salutes first, officer or enlisted?

Enlisted.

When the enlisted members salutes what else should take place?

Upon rendering the salute, the enlisted member is encouraged to initiate the proper greeting of the day. For example: Good Morning Sir/Ma'am.

When do enlisted members salute indoors?

When reporting to a superior officer.

Under what conditions does the Operator of military vehicles not render a salute?

When they are drivers of a moving vehicle.

When does an individual render a salute to a vehicle?

Upon individual identification of the superior's rank or by identifying vehicle plates or flags.

When is the national flag dipped?

It is never dipped by way of salute or compliment.

Funerals will be conducted in accordance with what manual?

TC 3-21.5 Chapter 14.

When uncased Colors pass by or when passing uncased Colors what action will a Soldier take?

When the Colors are approaching wait until they are at six paces from you and render present arms. Hold present arms until the Colors are six paces away.

At a military funeral, when is present arms executed?

At the command of the officer or NCO in charge and anytime the casket is moved.

Where did our military Customs come from?

They have been handed down over the centuries and add to the interest, pleasure and graciousness of Army life.

How will the flag be displayed on Memorial Day?

At half-staff from reveille until noon.

What is an Ensign?

A rectangular U.S. flag flown from an aircraft, ships, and boats.

What does the color Red symbolize on the Army flag?

Hardiness and Valor.

What does the color Blue symbolize on the Army flag?

Vigilance, Perseverance, and Justice.

What does the color White symbolize on the Army flag?

Purity and Innocence.

What color has been the unofficial color of the Army for more than 200 years?

Blue.

Who receives a 21-gun salute?

The President; Former President or President Elect; Sovereign or Chief of State of a Foreign Country or member of reigning royal family.

What is the lowest number of rounds fired for a Cannon salute for dignitaries?

11.

Sponsorship Program

AR 600-8-8

What regulations covers the Total Army Sponsorship Program?

AR 600-8-8.

Describe the elements of the Sponsorship program

Welcome letter; ACS relocation readiness services; reception; orientation; in processing; Garrison support.

What are the requirements for selecting a Sponsor?

The Soldier must be able to represent the unit in a positive manner.

Why is it important to select only qualified Sponsors?

They are the new Soldier's first impression of the unit.

Normally, who will not be selected as a Sponsor?

The Soldier being replaced by the incoming Soldier or a Soldier within 60 days of PCS.

Define Reactionary Sponsorship.

Sponsor support offered to a Soldier arriving at a unit without an assigned sponsor.

Define Rear Detachment Sponsorship.

Sponsor support provided to family members of a Soldier whose unit is deployed and is scheduled to return to the installation.

Substance Abuse Program

AR 600-85

What regulation covers the Army Substance Abuse Program?

AR 600-85.

What are the two overarching tenets of the ASAP program?

Prevention and treatment.

What action will be taken for a Soldier who fails to participate in or respond successfully to rehabilitation in the ASAP program?

They will be processed for separation from service.

What does the acronym ASAP stand for?

Army Substance Abuse Program.

When is a Soldier considered impaired by alcohol when on duty?

When the blood alcohol content is equal to or greater than .50 grams of alcohol per 100 milliliters of blood.

What action will be taken for a Soldier who is found to be drinking underage?

They will be referred to ASAP for screening within five days.

Define an ASAP Rehabilitation Failure.

Includes Soldiers with a subsequent alcohol or drug related incident of misconduct at any time during the 12 months period following successful completion of ASAP or during the 12-month period following removal from the program.

How much time will a Soldier have to report for testing once notified?

Two hours.

If a Soldier reports to the testing area, when or how are they allowed to depart the testing area?

Only when authorized by the commander to do so and they should be provided an NCO or Officer escort while away from the testing area.

What does the acronym UPL stand for?

Unit Prevention Leader.

What actions are directed for a Soldier that cannot provide a sample?

They should drink at least 8 ounces of fluid every half hour, not to exceed 40 ounces. Soldiers will remain in the holding area until they are ready to provide a specimen.

When a Soldier is informed, they will provide a sample what does this constitute?

A lawful order.

What are the methods of referral for the ASAP program?

Voluntary (Self ID); commander directed; drug testing ID; alcohol testing ID; medical ID; or investigation/apprehension.

What is the most desirable method of referral to the ASAP program?

Self-referral.

What are the rehabilitation levels?

Level 1: nonresidential/outpatient rehab; Level 2: partial inpatient/residential treatment.

Define the limited use policy.

Facilitates self-identification and allows a Soldier to get help and make a new start without being punished for past offenses.

What is the window a commander can provide for reporting to the testing station?

Within two hours of notification but no more than six hours.

Define that term "smart testing".

Random testing conducted in such a manner that is unpredictable by the testing population.

Supply

....

AR 735-5, AR 710-2, TC 3-27.76, TC 7-21.13, TC 7-22.7

What does CSDP stand for?

Command Supply Discipline Program.

Define CSDP.

A commander's program which leaders enforce to ensure resources are not subject to fraud, waste and abuse.

Who is responsible for enforcing the CSDP?

It is an individual, supervisory, and managerial responsibility.

Can government property be sold, given as a gift, loaned, exchanged, used for private purposes or otherwise be disposed of?

No.

Define Supply discipline.

The compliance with established DA regulations to effectively administer supply economy. Supply discipline applies to all functions and levels of supply (from unit/contractor through national users) and to the effective use of supply funds.

What is contained in Class I?

Food rations and water.

What is contained in Class III?

Fuel, oils and lubricants.

What is contained in Class V?

Ammunition.

Define Property Accountability.

It is the use, care, custody, and safekeeping of Organizational Clothing and Individual Equipment.

What does OCIE stand for?

Organizational Clothing and Individual Equipment.

What are the classifications of Army property?

Nonexpendable property; expendable property; durable property.

What are the types of property?

Organizational and Installation.

What are the five types of responsibility for CSDP?

Command; Supervisory, Direct; Custodial; Personal.

What does the acronym FLIPL stand for?

Financial Liability Investigation of Property Loss.

What is a FLIPL?

It is the manner in which the Army accounts for the circumstances surrounding the loss, damage, or destruction of government property.

Define Supply economy.

The conservation of material by every individual dealing with Army supplies to ensure that only the proper item in the necessary amount is used to accomplish a task. The term stewardship of resources is synonymous with supply economy.

When the hand receipt holder is replaced how long does the primary hand receipt holder have to conduct a joint inventory?

30 days.

How often are sensitive items inventoried?

Quarterly; with no more than one quarter of a year between inventories.

What is the DA FORM 2062?

Hand Receipt/Annex Number.

Schools

....

AR 350-1

What is the goal of NCO training and the NCOES?

To prepare NCOs to lead and train Soldiers who work and fight under their supervision, and assist their leaders in executing the mission.

If a Soldier fails their initial APFT test upon enrolling in a school, how long do they have to retake the APFT?

No earlier than seven days and no later than 24 days.

What does the BLC training course focus on?

Branch immaterial leadership training.

What does the ALC training course focus on?

Leader training and basic branch specific platoon and company level training.

What does the SLC training course focus on?

Advanced, branch-specific, platoon and company-level training.

What level of Self Development training is mandatory before attending BLC?

SSD1.

What level of Self Development training is mandatory before attending ALC?

SSD2.

What level of Self Development training is mandatory before attending SLC?

SSD3.

What Army Directive redesigned the Army Profile System?

Army Directive 2016-07.

What document does a Soldier receive upon graduation of a PME course?

DA form 1059.

What does the acronym NCOPDS stand for?

Noncommissioned Officer Professional Development System.

What does the acronym SSD stand for?

Structured Self-Development.

What action will be taken if a Soldier fails the APFT while enrolled in PME?

The Soldier will be removed from the course.

What action is taken if a Soldier attending PME does not meet the height and weight standard?

They are authorized one rescreening and it must be administered no earlier than seven days and no later than 24 days after the initial failure to meet the standard.

Name the four types of deferments for PME?

Compassionate, medical, operational, and noncommissioned officer evaluation system deferment process.

Training

ADRP 7-0, ADP 7-0, TC 7-21.13, TC 7-22.7

What subject does ADP 7-0 cover?

Training Units and developing leaders.

What ADP covers training units and developing leaders?

ADP 7-0.

According to ADP 7-0, what is the Army's life-blood?

Unit training and leader development.

Who is responsible for training units?

Commanders.

Name three principles of unit training.

Commanders and other leaders are responsible for training, NCO's train individuals, crews, and small teams, Train to standard, Train as you will fight, Train while operating, Train fundamentals first, Train to develop adaptability, Understand the operational environment, Train to sustain, Train to maintain, Conduct multi-echelon and concurrent training.

Name three principles of leader development.

Lead by example, Develop subordinate leaders, Create a learning environment for subordinate leaders, Train leaders in the art and science of mission command, Train to develop adaptive leaders, Train leaders to think critically and creatively, Train your leaders to know their subordinates and their families.

What does METL stand for?

Mission Essential Task List.

What is the institutional training domain?

The Army's institutional training and education system, which primarily includes training base centers and schools that provide initial training and subsequent professional military education for Soldiers, military leaders, and Army civilians.

What is the operational training domain?

The training activities organizations undertake while at home station, at maneuver combat training centers, during joint exercises, at mobilization centers, and while operationally deployed.

What is the subject of ADRP 7-0?

Training Units and Developing Leaders.

What is the self-development training domain?

Planned, goal-oriented learning that reinforces and expands the depth and breadth of an individual's knowledge base, self-awareness, and situational awareness; complements institutional and operational learning; enhances professional competence; and meets personal objectives.

What ADRP covers training units and developing leaders?

ADRP 7-0.

What does it mean by "train as you will fight"?

Training under an expected operational environment for the mission.

What format do Warning Orders follow?

The five paragraph OPORD format.

What does OPORD stand for?

Operations Order.

What is an After-Action Review (AAR)?

A guided analysis of an organization's performance, conducted at appropriate times during and at the conclusion of a training event or operation with the objective of improving future performance.

What does COA stand for?

Course of Action.

Define training objective.

A statement that describes the desired outcome of a training activity in the unit.

What regulation covers Army training leader development?

AR 350-1.

What does the acronym TADSS stand for?

Training Aids, Devices, Simulators, and Simulations.

What training domain bridges the gap between other training domains and sets the conditions for continuous learning and growth?

Self-development domain.

What commanders are considered primary trainers?

Company commanders.

What does the abbreviation ACT stand for?

Army Career Tracker.

How often will a Soldier's IDP and Army career tracker be reviewed?

It will be reviewed annually until the Soldier transitions from military service.

What elements are used to standardize Army training?

Army task, conditions, and standards.

What reference and tools are used to manage unit training?

FM 7-0 and ATMS (DTMS).

What regulation covers the policies that govern the Army physical fitness training program?

AR 350-1.

Who are the principal trainers of individual Soldiers?

NCOs.

Define METL.

A compilation of mission essential tasks that a unit performs based on its design, equipment, manning and table of organization and equipment/distribution and allowance and its mission.

Define Individual Tasks.

It supports one or more collective tasks or drills and often supports another individual task.

Define Collective Tasks.

They are clearly defined observable, and measurable activities or actions that require organized team or unit performance.

What are the three domains of Soldier Development?

(1) The Institutional domain; (2) Operational domain; (3)The Self Development domain

Explain the Army Training Network.

Provides on-line self-help services such as doctrine, references, and training products.

What does ATN stand for?

Army Training Network.

What is Army Career Tracker?

An individual career management system aimed at supporting the lifecycle of the Soldiers.

What is the primary focus of a unit when not deployed?

Training.

Who are the primary trainers of enlisted Soldiers, crews, and small teams?

NCOs.

How is lifelong learned managed in the Army?

Through the Army Career Tracker.

Provide an example of institutional domain training.

MOS specific education.

Provide an example of operational domain training.

Training activities done at the unit or during major exercises; individual tasks; and mandatory training.

Define NCODP.

Session tailored to unique unit requirements and support the commander's leader training and leader development program.

Name the three types of self-development.

Structured; guided; personal self-development.

Define an After-Action Review.

It is a structured review process that allows participants to discover how and why certain events actually happened and how to improve future task performance.

Uniforms

AR 670-1, DA PAM 670-1

What Army regulation covers Wear and Appearance of the Army Uniforms and Insignia?

AR 670-1.

AR 670-1 states that some portions of the regulation are punitive in nature. What does this mean?

It means Soldiers can be punished under the UCMJ for failing to follow the specified procedures.

How will leaders judge the appropriateness of a hairstyle?

By the ability to wear all types of headgear (such as beret, patrol cap, or service cap/hat) and any protective equipment (such as protective mask or combat helmet) properly.

When using dyes, tints, or bleaches on the hair, what must a Soldier ensure?

It must be a natural hair color.

What are the three categories of female hairstyles?

Short, medium, and long length.

What is the maximum fingernail length for a female Soldier?

1/4 of an inch.

What types of tattoos and brands are prohibited?

Extremist, indecent, sexist, or racist.

On what part of the body are tattoos or brands prohibited?

Head or face.

When are Soldiers authorized to cover tattoos with bandages or makeup to comply with AR 670-1 requirements?

Never.

What items of jewelry is a Soldier authorized to wear?

1. Wristwatch
2. A wrist religious or identification bracelet
3. A total of two rings (a wedding set is considered one ring).
4. Soldiers may also wear one activity tracker, pedometer, or heart rate monitor with Army uniforms.
5. Bracelets are limited to medical alert bracelets, missing in action, prisoner of war, killed in action (black or silver color only), and religious bracelets similar in size and appearance to identification bracelets.

What is an authorized storage location for headgear in the Class C uniform?

The cargo pocket and the small of the back with the bill tucked in the belt.

Describe the female short hair style.

Short hair is defined as hair length that extends no more than 1 inch from the scalp (excluding bangs). Hair may be no shorter than 1/4 inch from the scalp (unless due to medical condition or injury), but may be evenly tapered to the scalp within 2 inches of the hair line edges. Bangs, if worn, may not fall below the eyebrows, may not interfere with the wear of all headgear, must lie neatly against the head, and not be visible underneath the front of the headgear. The width of the bangs may extend to the hairline at the temple. *Change Per ALARACT 015/2021 States: There is no minimum hair length for female soldiers. The hair may have a tapered appearance and if the hair does not part naturally, the soldier may cut a part into the hair, or style the hair with one part. The part will be one straight line, not slanted or curved, and will fall in the area where the soldier would normally part the hair. Soldiers will not shape or cut designs into their hair or scalp.*

Describe the female medium hair style.

Medium hair is defined as hair length that does not extend beyond the lower edge of the collar (in all uniforms), and extends more than 1 inch from the scalp. Medium hair may fall naturally in uniform, and is not required to be secured. When worn loose, graduated hair styles are acceptable, but the length, as measured from the end of the total hair length to the base of the collar, may not exceed 1 inch difference in length, from the front to the back. Layered hairstyles are also authorized, so long as each hair's length, as measured from the scalp to the hair's end, is generally the same length giving a tapered appearance. The regulations for the wear of bangs detailed in para-graph 3–2a(3)(a), apply. No portion of the bulk of the hair, as measured from the scalp, will exceed 2 inches. *Change Per ALARACT 015/2021 States: Authorizes medium length ponytails for female soldiers who are unable to form a bun due to length and/or texture of hair. In all uniforms, the unsecured hair will be worn centered in the back of the head (placement of ponytail will not be on the side or top of the head), be no wider than the width of the head, will not extend beyond the lower edge of the collar, and will not interfere with proper wear of authorized army headgear.*

Describe the female long hair style.

Long hair is defined as hair length that extends beyond the lower edge of the collar. Long hair will be neatly and inconspicuously fastened or pinned above the lower edge of the collar (except when worn in accordance with para 3−2a(j)), except that bangs may be worn. The regulations for the wear of bangs detailed in para-graph 3−2a(3)(a) apply. No portion of the bulk of the hair, as measured from the scalp as styled, will exceed 2 inches (except a bun, which is worn on the back of the head and may extend a maximum of 3 1/2 inches from the scalp and be no wider than the width of the head). *Change Per ALARACT 015/2021 States: Authorizes female soldiers to wear long ponytails in utility uniforms when conducting physical training or tactical operations. While walking to and from the designated area of physical training (formation) the long ponytail is authorized. Additionally, while female soldiers are wearing equipment such as, but not limited to, combat vehicle crewman (cvc) or advanced combat helmets (ach), they will be authorized to wear their hair in a ponytail and/ or a long braid secured in their utility uniform top.*

Describe the multiple hairstyles.

Braids, cornrows, twists, and locks. Medium and long hair may be styled with braids, cornrows, twists, or locks (see glossary for definitions). Each braid, cornrow, twist, or lock will be of uniform dimension, have a diameter no greater than a 1/2 inch, and present a neat, professional, and well-groomed appearance. Each must have the same approximate size of spacing between the braids, cornrows, twists, or locks. Each hairstyle may be worn against the scalp or loose (free-hanging). When worn loose, such hairstyles must be worn per medium hair length guidelines or secured to the head in the same manner as described for medium or long length hair styles. Ends must be secured inconspicuously. When multiple loose braids, twists, or locks are worn, they must encompass the whole head. When braids, cornrows, twists, or locks are not worn loosely and instead worn close to the scalp, they must stop at one consistent location of the head and must follow the natural direction of the hair when worn back, which is either in general straight lines following the shape of the head or flowing with the natural direction of the hair when worn back with one primary part in the hair (see para 3–2a(1) (c)). Hairstyles may not be styled with designs, sharply curved lines, or zigzag lines. Only one distinctive style (braided, rolled, twisted, or locked) may be worn at one time. Braids, cornrows, twists, or locks that distinctly protrude (up or out) from the head are not authorized. The bulk of the hair may not be such that it impairs the ability to wear the advanced combat helmet (ACH) or other protective equipment or impedes the ability to operate one's assigned weapon, military equipment, or machinery. A fully serviceable ACH including all of its component parts must be worn in accordance with its technical manual to ensure a proper fit for safety. *Change Per ALARACT 015/2021 States: Authorizes female soldiers to wear "multiple" hairstyles at once as long as they are neat in appearance and do not impact the proper wear of headgear and equipment. For example, braided twists or loc hair style with a side twist to secure hair, placed in a ponytail or two single cornrows encompassing all the hair, going into a ponytail or a bun in the back of the head. Also, remove the restrictions of braids, cornrows, twists, and locs having the same dimensions and same approximate size of spacing between them.*

Describe the proper wear of a mustache.

When mustaches are permitted, they must be maintained to a length not to exceed 2 inches when measured from the bottom of the chin. Beard hair longer than 2 inches must be rolled and/or tied to achieve the required length. Beards must be worn in a neat and conservative manner that presents a professional appearance. Soldiers may use styling products to groom or hold the beard in place, but may not use petroleum-based products if wearing a protective mask during training. The bulk of a Soldier's beard may not impair the ability to operate an assigned weapon, military equipment, or machinery.

Describe the male hairstyle.

The hair on top of the head must be neatly groomed. The length and bulk of the hair may not be excessive and must present a neat and conservative appearance. The hair must present a tapered appearance. A tapered appearance is one where the outline of the Soldier's hair conforms to the shape of the head, curving inward to the natural termination point at the base of the neck. When the hair is combed, it will not fall over the ears or eyebrows, or touch the collar, except for the closely cut hair at the back of the neck. The block-cut fullness in the back is permitted to a moderate degree, as long as the tapered look is maintained. Males are not authorized to wear braids, cornrows, twists, dreadlocks, or locks while in uniform or in civilian clothes on duty. Hair-cuts with a single, untapered patch of hair on the top of the head (not consistent with natural hair loss) are considered eccentric and are not authorized. Examples include, but are not limited to, when the head is shaved around a strip of hair down the center of the head (mohawk), around a u-shaped hair area (horseshoe), or around a patch of hair on the front top of the head (tear drop). Hair that is completely shaved or trimmed closely to the scalp is authorized.

Describe how females will apply cosmetics.

Females are authorized to wear cosmetics with all uniforms, provided they are applied modestly and conservatively, and that they complement both the Soldier's complexion and the uniform. Leaders at all levels must exercise good judgment when interpreting and enforcing this policy.

When a Soldier is not in compliance with the tattoo or branding policy, what action must a commander take?

Counsel the Soldier in writing on a DA Form 4856.

Can a Soldier cut a part in their hair if no natural part exists? If so explain?

Soldiers who have a texture of hair that does not part naturally may cut a part into the hair or style the hair with one part. The part will be one straight line, not slanted or curved, and will fall in the area where the Soldier would normally part the hair. Soldiers will not shape or cut designs into their hair or scalp.

Describe proper wear of hair devices and give three examples of authorized hair devices.

Hair holding devices are authorized only for the purpose of securing the hair. Soldiers will not place hair holding devices in the hair for decorative purposes. All hair holding devices must be plain and of a color as close to the Soldier's hair as is possible or clear. Authorized devices include, but are not limited to, small plain scrunchies (elastic hair bands covered with material), barrettes, combs, pins, clips, rubber bands, and hair or head bands. Such devices should conform to the natural shape of the head.

What requirements will female Soldiers comply with when wearing lipstick?

Females will not wear shades of lipstick that distinctly contrast with the natural color of their lips, that detract from the uniform, or that are faddish, eccentric, or exaggerated. *Change Per ALARACT 015/2021 States: Authorizes female soldiers to wear solid color shades of lipstick that are not extreme. Extreme colors include, but are not limited to; purple, bright pink, bright red, gold, blue, black, hot pink, green, yellow, ombre and fluorescent/neon colors. Natural colors, to include tinted glasses, are authorized. The optional wear of lip liner is authorized, but colors must match the shade of lipstick being worn.*

What is the policy concerning affixing, displaying articles of jewelry or ornamentation to, thru, or under the skin or any other body part?

This practice is prohibited.

What are the requirements for wearing religious jewelry in uniform?

Soldiers may wear religious items that are not visible or apparent when in duty uniform, provided they do not interfere with the performance of the Soldier's military duties or interfere with the proper wearing of any authorized article of the uniform.

What items of jewelry cannot be worn on the foot?

Toe rings and ankle bracelets.

What type of socks are authorized with the PT uniform?

Plain white or black socks calf or ankle-length.

What manuals cover wear and appearance of the uniform?

AR 670-1 and DA PAM 670-1.

How is the distinctive unit insignia worn on the male Army service uniform?

Centered on the shoulder loops and equal distance from the outside shoulder seam to the outside edge of the button with the base of the insignia towards the outside shoulder seam.

How is the insignia grade worn on the male Army service uniform?

Centered between the shoulder seam and the elbow. When the position of the shoulder sleeve insignia does not allow for proper placement of the Grade insignia is placed 1/2 inch below the SSI.

How is one marksmanship or skill badge worn on the male Army service uniform?

Center the marksmanship badge on the pocket flap 1/8 of an inch below the top of the pocket.

How is the nameplate worn on the male Army Green Service Uniform?

Center the nameplate on the flap of the right pocket between the top of the button and the top of the pocket.

How are the US and branch insignias worn on the male Army Green Service Uniform?

Place the bottom edge of the disk approximately one inch above the notch, centered on the collar with the centerline of the insignia parallel to the inside edge of the lapel.

What does the acronym IPFU stand for?

Improved Physical Fitness Uniform.

How are foreign badges worn on a male Soldier's Army Green Service Uniform?

Wear the foreign badge centered an 1/8 inch above the right pocket flap, or 1/2 inch above any unit awards that are worn. Personnel may not wear a foreign badge unless at least one U.S. medal or service ribbon is worn at the same time. Foreign badges are not authorized for wear on mess or utility uniforms. Personnel may not wear foreign badges that are awarded only as cloth badges. Personnel may not wear foreign badges that cannot be worn properly because of size or configuration.

Weapons

....

TC 21-3

What lubricant should be used on your weapon during cold weather operations?

CLP.

Using CLP on a weapon in cold weather operations helps prevent the weapon from ___.

Sweating.

Fratricide

....

TC 3-22.19

Name two of the four fratricide prevention methods?

Markings, panels (VS-17), lighting, beacons and strobes.

What is Rule four as it pertains to firearms safety and fratricide prevention?

Ensure positive identification of the target and its surroundings.

What two processes can leaders implement to help prevent fratricide and collateral damage?

Weapons Control Status, and Weapon Safety Status.

Range Card

TC 3-21.75, TC 3-22.19

What does FPL stand for?

Final Protective Line.

Define an FPL.

A predetermined line along which grazing fire is placed to stop an enemy assault.

Define grazing fire.

Occurs when the center of the cone of fire rises less than one meter above the ground.

What is plunging fire?

Occurs when the danger space is within the beaten zone.

What is dead space?

An area that direct fire weapons cannot hit.

What is a sector of fire?

An area to be covered by fire that is assigned to an individual, a weapon, or unit.

What are the four elements of a Range Card?

Sector of fire, principal direction of fire, final protective line, and dead space.

Tripod

....

TC 3-22.19

What does the abbreviation T&E stand for?

Traversing and Elevating Mechanism.

What is the purpose of a T&E mechanism?

Used to engage pre-selected target areas.

What is the weight of the M3 tripod?

44 LBS.

What is the weight of the M205 tripod?

34 LBS.

Grenades

....

TC 3-21.75, TC 3-23.30

What are the three categories of hand grenades?

Stun, concussion, and fragmentation.

What manual covers Grenades and Pyrotechnic Signals?

TC 3-23.30.

Name three of the six types of hand grenades.

Fragmentation; chemical, offensive; nonlethal; smoke; practice and training.

What does the acronym TPG stand for?

Training Practice Grenade.

How long is the fuse delay on the M228 TPF?

Four to five seconds.

What is the most commonly used fragmentation grenade?

The M67.

How long is the fuse delay on the M67 fragmentation grenade?

4-5.5 seconds.

What is the average throwing distance of the M67 fragmentation grenade?

35 meters.

What is the effective casualty producing radius of the M67 fragmentation grenade?

15 meters.

What is the killing radius of the M67 fragmentation grenade?

Five meters.

What is the purpose of the MK3A2 offensive hand grenade?

They are used for concussion effects in enclosed areas; blasting and for demolition tasks.

When is the MK3A2 offensive hand grenade most effective?

Against enemy Soldiers located in bunkers, buildings, and fortified areas.

What is the effective casualty producing radius of the MK3A2 offensive hand grenade?

Two meters in open areas.

How long is the fuse delay of the M84 stun grenade?

1-2.3 seconds.

What is the throwing distance of the M84 stun grenade?

40 meters.

What is the effective casualty producing results of the M84 stun grenade?

Temporary loss of hearing within nine meters and up to three seconds of flash blindness.

What is the primary purpose of chemical grenades?

Incendiary purposes and riot control.

What is the AN-M14TH3 hand grenade used for?

To destroy equipment; it can also damage, immobilize, or destroy vehicles, weapons systems, shelters, or munitions.

How long is the fuse delay of the AN-M14TH3 incendiary hand grenade?

.7-2.0 seconds.

What are the effects of the AN-M14TH3 incendiary hand grenade?

It burns at 4,330 degrees Fahrenheit; can burn through 1/8th inch steel plate; produces its own oxygen and burns under water.

What is the throwing distance of the AN-M14TH3 incendiary hand grenade?

25 meters.

What is the purpose of the M7A3CS grenade?

Riot control.

How long is the fuse delay for the M7A3CS riot control grenade?

.7-2.0 seconds.

What is the throwing distance of the M7A3CS riot control hand grenade?

40 meters.

What are the effects of the M7A3CS riot control grenade?

Produces a cloud of irritant agent for 15-35 seconds.

What are chemical grenades used for?

Incendiary purposes; screening; signaling; training; or riot control.

Mines

Land Mine

....

TC 3-21.75

When probing for mines, how far apart should you probe?

About every two inches.

When probing for mines, at what angle should the probe be used?

Less than 45 degrees.

What is the M-131?

Modular Pack Mine System. A man portable antitank and antipersonnel mine system.

What is the M21 mine used for?

Anti-tank mission.

What should you do before probing for mines?

Leave your load bearing equipment and rifle with another member of the team. Keep your helmet and body armor on to protect from possible blast.

What device can be used to probe for mines?

A wooden stick at least 12 inches long.

What must you do to one end of your wooden probe?

Sharpen it.

How wide of a lane should the Soldier create as they clear the minefield?

A 1-meter wide path.

M18A1

....

TC 3-21.75, TC 3-22.23

When using the knife edge site on the M18 Claymore mine, how should it be aimed?

50 meters out at the base of your target area.

When using the peep sight on the M18 Claymore mine, how should it be aimed?

50 meters out, 8 feet above the ground.

What is the weight of the M18 Claymore mine?

3.5 lbs.

How many projectiles are packed into the M18 Claymore mine?

700.

What manual covers the use of the M18A1 Claymore Munition?

TC 3-22.23.

Describe the M18A1 Claymore Munition.

A directional, fixed fragmentation munition; primarily designed for use against massed infantry attacks; however, its fragments are also effective against light armored vehicles.

How far away should the Soldier be from an installed M18A1 before firing?

At least 50 meters.

What is the maximum effective range of the fragmentation from the M18A1?

Up to 100 meters.

What is the optimal effective range of the M18A1?

The optimal effective range for lethality and area coverage is 50 meters.

What type of munition is the M18A1?

Antipersonnel.

What types of sights are available on the M18A1?

Fixed plastic knife edge sight or slit type peep sight on earlier models.

What is the danger area when firing the M18A1?

180-degree fan with a radius of 250 meters centered in the direction of the aim.

What is the minimum safe operating distance of the M18A1?

16 meters.

When firing the M18A1, friendly troops must take cover within __ meters when the munition is fired.

100 meters.

What is the hazard to the operator and friendly troops when the M18A1 is detonated?

Injury by flying secondary objects such as sticks, stones, and pebbles.

The M18A1 has a curved surface. The outer surface has wording on it. In which direction should the side with the wording on it be placed?

Front towards enemy.

When aiming the M18A1 the operator should select an aiming point at ground level approximately __ meters in front of the munition.

50 meters or 150 feet.

How far to the rear of the M18A1 should the operator's eye be from the sight?

Approximately six inches.

Before firing the M18A1 what should the operator shout?

CLAYMORE, CLAYMORE.

Where should the firing device for the M18A1 be at all times?

On the operator's person at all time. This action is to protect you and all other personnel from accidentally or intentional denotation by an unauthorized person.

When conducting a circuit test with the M57 firing device and M40 test set, the operator will squeeze the handle of the M57 rapidly. What should the operator observe?

The operator should observe the indicator lamp and look for flashing in the window. If the device flashes the circuit is functioning properly.

When performing a circuit test where is the blasting cap placed?

Under a sandbag; behind a tree; in a hole, etc. This protects the Soldier performing the circuit test should the blasting cap accidentally detonate.

What type of fragmentation patterns does the M18A1 deliver?

Two meters high and 50 meters wide.

What is the maximum range of the fragmentation from the M18A1?

Up to 200 meters.

M2 .50 Cal

TC 3-22.50, TC 3-21.76

What subject does TC 3-22.50 cover?

M2 .50 caliber Heavy Machine Gun.

Describe the M2 .50 caliber Machine Gun

A belt fed, recoil operated, air cooled, crew served machine gun. Provides automatic suppressive fire for offensive and defensives purposes. Can be used against personnel, light armored vehicles, and low/slow flying aircraft. It can fire single shot and automatic, left- or right-hand feed. Can be ground mounted on tripods.

Can M2A1 parts be used on the M2?

No; Never install M2A1 parts on the M2 at operator level.

What is the weight of the M2/M2A1?

84 lbs.

What is the weight of the M2/M2A1 barrel?

26 lbs.

How is the M2/M2A1 cooled?

Air cooled.

What is the maximum range of the M2/M2A1?

7,400 yards.

What is the maximum effective range of the M2/M2A1?

2,000 yards.

What is the difference between the M2 and M2A1 when it comes to head spacing?

The M2 head space is manually set and checked; the M2A1 has a head space that is fixed.

Describe the operational function of the M2/M2A1

Feeding; chambering; locking; firing; unlocking; extracting; ejecting; and cocking.

What types of ammunition does the M2/M2A1 fire?

Ball, Tracer, Armor Piercing Incendiary, Plastic Practice Ball, Blank, Dummy.

How many major components are there to the M2 and M2A1?

8.

How many lands and grooves does the M2/M2A1 have?

8.

What is the twist and the ratio of the M2/M2A1 barrel?

Right hand twist; 1 turn in 15 inches.

How is the M2/M2A1 fed?

Link belt.

How does the M2/M2A1 operate/function?

Recoil operated.

What is the muzzle velocity of the M2/M2A1?

3,050 ft per second.

What type of rear sight does the M2 have?

Leaf type rear sight.

The rear sight of the M2 ranges from 100 yards to __yards.

2,600 yards.

What does T&E stand for?

Traversing and Elevation Mechanism.

What is the nomenclature for the M2 lightweight Machine Gun Tripod?

M205.

What is the weight of the M205 tripod?

34 lbs.

What is a cone of fire?

The slightly different trajectories formed by a single burst is called the cone of fire.

What is the beaten zone?

An elliptical pattern formed by the cone of fire as it strikes the ground.

The battle sight zero for M2 is fixed at ___ yards.

750 yards.

What are the three methods for cooling the M2/M2A1?

Radiational; conduction; convection.

What is the weight of the M2 with barrel and tripod?

128 lbs.

What is the maximum effective range of the M2 point target single shot?

1500 meters.

What is the maximum effective range of the M2 for an area target?

1830 meters.

What is the maximum effective range of the M2 for grazing fire?

700 meters.

What is the tracer burnout for the M2?

1800 meters.

What is the sustained rate of fire for the M2?

40 rpm, 6-9 rounds, 10-15 seconds.

What is the rapid rate of fire for the M2?

40 rpm, 6-9 rounds, 5-10 seconds.

What is the cyclic rate of fire for the M2?

450-550 rpm continuous burst.

M4/M16

STP 21-1, TC 3-22.9, TC 3-21.75

What is the first step in handling a weapon?

Clear It.

The acronym SPORTS stand for?

Slap, pull, observe, release, tap, shoot.

How should you adjust the front sight post on the M4 for mechanical zero?

Flush with the front sight post housing.

How should you adjust the elevation knob on the rear sight for mechanical zero?

Align the index mark with the 6/3 marking.

Name two weapons that can be attached to the M4 carbine?

Grenade launcher (M203) and shotgun (M26).

When multiple targets of the same threat level are encountered what is the order of engagement?

Near before far, front before flank, and stationary before moving.

Describe how to perform a function check on an M4.

Clear weapon, place on safe, pull charging handle to rear, release, pull trigger, hammer should not fall, place selector on SEMI, pull trigger, hammer should fall, hold trigger to rear and charge weapon, release trigger with a slow smooth motion, until trigger is fully forward, listen for audible click, pull trigger, hammer should fall, place selector on BURST, charge weapon one time, hammer should fall, hold trigger to the rear, charge weapon three times, release trigger, squeeze trigger, hammer should fall.

Name two of the four malfunctions remedial action can correct.

Stovepipe, double feed, bolt over ride, charging handle impingement.

What are the two methods for defeating moving targets?

Tracking and trapping.

What are the elements of the zero process?

Mechanical zero, laser bore light, 25 m grouping and zeroing, and zero confirmation out to 300 meters.

What manual covers the M4 and M16 weapon systems?

TC 3 22.9.

Describe the M4/M-16 series weapon.

5.56 mm, magazine fed, gas operated, air cooled, shoulder fired rifle or carbine, with semiautomatic, three round burst capability, or earlier version have automatic capability.

Describe the cycle of functioning.

Feeding, chambering, locking, firing, unlocking, extracting, ejecting, and cocking.

What is the name of TC 3 22.9?

Rifle and carbine.

What are the two types of corrective action?

Immediate action and remedial action.

What are the three methods of cooling?

Radiation, conduction, and convection cooling.

What does the acronym BUIS stand for?

Backup iron site.

What three elements must a Soldier master in order to hit a target?

Site alignment, site picture, and trigger control.

Define malfunction.

When a weapon fails to complete any phase of the cycle of function correctly.

Name three of the five types of malfunctions.

Failure to fire, failure to feed, failure to chamber, failure to extract, failure to eject.

Define cookoff.

When a round fires because the weapon has overheated.

Name the seven types of ammunition used by the M4.

Ball, Tracer, Armor Piercing, Blank, Close Combat Mission Capability Kit, Dummy, Short-Range Training.

Define Battle sight Zero.

The alignment of the sights with the weapon's barrel given standard issue ammunition.

What is the weight of the M4 with sling and one loaded magazine?

7.5 LBS.

What is the maximum effective range of the M4 on an area target?

600 meters.

When preparing to mechanical zero the M4, which aperture is facing up?

The unmarked aperture.

What is reflexive fire?

Automatic trained response to fire your weapon with minimal reaction time, it allows for little or no margin of error.

What is remedial action?

A skilled, technique that must be applied to a specific problem or issue with the weapon that will not be corrected by taking immediate action. Remedial action is taken when the cycle of function is interrupted where the trigger is squeezed and either has little resistance during the squeeze ("mush") or the trigger cannot be squeezed.

What are the proper steps to mechanical zero the M4 series rifle/carbine?

Set rear apertures by positioning the apertures so the unmarked aperture is up and the 0-200-meter aperture is down. Set windage by turning the windage knob to align the index mark on the 0-200-meter aperture with the long center index line on the rear sight assembly. Turn the elevation knob counterclockwise until the rear sight assembly rests flush with the detachable carrying handle and the 6 / 3 marking is aligned with the index line on the left side of the carrying handle.

Turning the front sight post of the M4 series rifle clockwise will move the strike of the bullet in which direction?

Clockwise moves the strike of the bullet down.

What is the maximum range of the M4 series rifle?

3600 meters.

What is the muzzle velocity of the M4 series rifle?

2970 feet per second.

MK19

....

TC 3-22.19, TC 3-21.76

What subject does TC 3-22.19 cover?

Mark 19 Grenade Launcher.

Describe the MK19 grenade launcher.

An air cooled, blowback operated machine gun that is belt fed with six major assemblies.

What is the cycling or firing process of the MK19?

Charging, extracting, cocking, firing, recoil, and automatic feeding.

When engaging a target and looking through the sights, what should the gunner focus on?

The front sight post not the target itself.

What type of ammunition does the MK19 fire?

Target practice, high explosive, high explosive dual purpose, dummy, or HVCC.

What is the purpose of the High Velocity Canister Cartridge round for the MK19?

Used only to produce anti-personnel effects on the battlefield, should not be used against lightly armored vehicles.

At what distance is a field zero performed when using the MK19?

400 meters.

How many major components are there to the MK19?

6.

What is the weight of the MK19 without the feed throat?

77.6 LBS.

What is the weight of the MK19 with the feed throat?

78 LBS.

What are the major components of the MK19?

Bolt and backplate assembly, receiver assembly, feed slide assembly and tray, top cover assembly, feed throat assembly, sear assembly.

What FM covers the MK19 Grenade Launcher?

FM 3-22.27.

What is the weight of the MK19 with barrel and tripod?

140.6 lbs.

What is the maximum effective range of the MK19 for a point target?

1500 meters.

What is the maximum effective range of the MK19 for an area target?

2212 meters.

What is the sustained rate of fire for the MK19?

40 rpm.

What is the rapid rate of fire for the MK19?

60 rpm.

What is the cyclic rate of fire for the MK19?

325-375 rpm, continuous burst.

What is unique about the MK19's barrel?

It is designed not to overheat.

M26 Shotgun

TC 3-22.12

What subject does TC 3-22.12 cover?

M26 Modular Accessory Shotgun System.

Why was the M26 M4 Mountable Shotgun developed?

It eliminated the need for Soldiers to transition from one weapon system to another.

What does the M26 Shotgun allow Soldiers to do when properly employed?

Employ lethal, non-lethal shotgun munitions during low-intensity operations or perform ballistic breaching tasks.

Describe the M2 Modular Shotgun.

Box magazine fed, manually operated 12-gauge shotgun with a straight push pull action, mounted under the M4/M4A1 carbine.

What size rounds does the M26 Shotgun use?

2 3/4 to 3-inch magnum range.

What does the acronym MASS stand for?

Modular Accessory Shotgun System.

How many rounds can the 26 MASS hold?

Six; five rounds in the magazine and one round in the chamber.

What type of lethal ammunition does the M26 MASS fire?

00 buckshot; # 7.5; # 9 birdshot; and breaching rounds.

With regard to the M26 MASS, during clearing procedures what must the gunner ensure?

Ensure the weapon is on SAFE.

With regard to the M26 MASS, how should cleaning patches be run through the muzzle?

Breach to muzzle.

What is considered an extremely serious failure of the M26 MASS?

Failure to extract.

What is the maximum effective range of the M26 MASS Non-lethal round?

20 meters (66 ft).

What is the maximum effective range of the M26 MASS Buckshot ammunition?

40 meters (131 ft).

What is the maximum effective range of the M26 MASS Breaching rounds?

0 to 3 inches (0-76 cm).

With regard to the M26 MASS, what is the maximum range of the M162 00 buckshot?

175 meters.

With regard to the M26 MASS, what is the maximum range of the M1030 breaching cartridge?

175 meters.

With regard to the M26 MASS, what is the maximum effective range of the M1030 breaching cartridge?

5 meters.

With regard to the M26 MASS, what is the purpose of the weapon using the M162 00 buckshot?

Medium to close range work up to 30 meters; anti-personnel use for guard in combat.

With regard to the M26 MASS, what is the advantage of using the M162 00 buckshot round?

Retains energy longer; lethal at a longer range.

If a round fails to function, what action should be taken with that round?

Dispose of in accordance with unit SOP and ensure it is reported and returned to the unit that issued the ammunition.

What is the weight of the M26 MASS?

Mounted 3. 5 lbs.; stand-alone 5.3 lbs.

What is the muzzle velocity of the M26 MASSS?

It is ammunition specific.

Name three of the accessories that come with the M26 MASS.

Adjustable sling; operator cleaning and maintenance kit; pistol grip; buttstock and grip assembly. Five round magazines; five 3 round magazines; one magazine pouch; 1 receiver plug; and 1 upper mounting bracket.

M72 Light Anti-Tank Weapon

TC 3-21.75

What is the maximum effective range of the M72 LAW?

220 meters.

What is the minimum range for the M72 LAW?

20 meters.

What is the caliber of the M72 LAW?

66mm.

What is the weight of the M72 LAW?

2.2 lbs.

What is the minimum arming distance of the M72 LAW?

10 meters.

What is the maximum range of the M72 LAW?

1,000 meters.

M136/AT4

What is the maximum effective range of the M136 AT4?

300 meters.

What is the minimum safe target engagement range of the M136 AT4?

15 meters.

What is the major concern when firing an AT4 from a fighting position?

The back blast could cause friendly casualties.

What is the caliber of the M136 AT4?

84mm.

What is the weight of the M136 AT4?

14.8 lbs.

What is the AT4CS?

An enhanced version of the AT4 that allows it to be fired from a confined space, room, or protected enclosure.

What action will a Soldier, in combat, take if the AT4 malfunctions and corrective action fails?

Break off the sites of the weapon so it can easily identify as unserviceable.

What are the minimum safe target engagement range for the AT4 in combat?

15 meters.

What is the maximum range of the M136 AT4?

2,297 yards.

Describe the M136 AT4?

The M136 AT4 is a lightweight, self-contained, anti-armor weapon. It consists of a free-flight, fin-stabilized, rocket-type cartridge packed in an expendable, one-piece, fiberglass-wrapped tube. The AT4 is man-portable and is fired from the right shoulder only.

Can the M136 AT4 be fired from either shoulder?

It can only be fired from the right shoulder.

M141 Bunker Defeat Munition

TC 3-21.75

What is the M141 BDM?

Bunker Defeat Munition.

What is the maximum effective range of the M141 BDM?

300 meters.

What is the minimum arming range of the M141 BDM?

15 meters.

What is the caliber of the M141 BDM?

83mm.

How much does the M141 BDM weigh?

15.7 lbs.

M203 40 mm Grenade Launcher

TC 3-21.75

What is the caliber of the M203?

40mm.

What is the maximum effective range of the M203 on an area target?

350 meters.

What is the maximum effective range of the M203 on a point target?

150 meters.

What is the weight of the M203?

3 lbs. empty / 3.6 lbs. loaded.

What is the rate of fire of the M203?

Five to seven rounds per minute.

M320 40 mm Grenade Launcher

TC 3-22.31

What manual covers the M320?

TM 3-22.31.

What is the significance of the M320?

It is replacing the M203.

What is the weight of M320 without the buttstock?

5lbs.

What is the weight of M320 with the buttstock?

7lbs.

What is the muzzle velocity of the M320?

236.22 feet per second.

What is the maximum effective range of the M320 on an area target?

350 meters.

What is the maximum effective range of the M320 on a point target?

150 meters.

What is the maximum range of the M320?

400 meters.

What type of rounds can the M320 fire?

Training Practice Round, High Explosive Service Round, Non-Lethal Cartridge, Pyrotechnic Signal and Spotting Rounds.

Name the approved methods of destroying the M320.

Mechanical, Burning, Demolition, and Disposal.

Describe the disposal destruction method for the M320.

Bury essential parts, dump them in streams, or scatter them so widely that recovering them would be impossible.

What is the danger radius of the practice grenade?

20 meters.

What is the danger radius of the HE Service Round?

165 meters.

What are the stoppages associated with the M320?

Failure to Fire, Failure to Eject, Failure to Extract, and Failure to Chamber.

You have pulled the trigger on the M320 and the weapon did not fire. How will you determine if the weapons or the munition is defective?

If the primer of the round is dented the munition is faulty, if the primer is not dented then the weapon is faulty.

What type of HE rounds can the M320 fire?

Standard HE service round and the HEDP Service round.

How do you conduct a function check on the M320?

(1) Clear the host weapon. (2) Clear the grenade launcher. (3) Rotate the selector lever from the SAFE ("S") to the FIRE ("F") position and back to the SAFE ("S") position with an audible click. (4) With the selector lever in SAFE ("S") position, attempt to pull the trigger rearward. The trigger must remain in the forward position (no rearward travel). (5) Press the barrel release, and allow the barrel to pivot outward. (6) Place the selector lever in SAFE ("S") position. (7) Ensure that the firing pin located on the hammer does not protrude from the bolt face into the chamber. (8) Move the selector lever to the FIRE ("F") position. (9) Press the barrel release while attempting to pull the trigger. It must not be possible to pull the trigger enough to raise and release the hammer. (10) With the barrel pivoted outward and the selector lever in the FIRE ("F") position, pull the trigger, and press the finger lightly on the breech face to detect the firing pin protrusion.

Describe the M320/M320A1 grenade launcher.

It is a lightweight grenade launcher that can operate in a standalone or attached configuration. It uses a double-action-only trigger system. It can accurately engage targets as far away as 350 meters. It has ambidextrous operating controls and a sling mounting point allow the weapon to be fitted to the Soldier. The swing out barrel aids the Soldier in rapid reloading.

M240B Machine Gun

TC 3-22.240

What subject does TC 3-22.240 cover?

Medium Machine Gun 240.

Why should the gunner never open the feed tray cover on a hot gun?

An open cover cook off could damage the weapon and result in serious injury to the firer.

Describe the M240 (detailed description)?

Gas operated, belt fed, air cooled, fully automatic, and firing from the open bolt position.

How many major components are there for the M240?

8.

Name in order the phases of the cycle of function for the M240.

Feeding, chambering, locking, firing, unlocking, extracting, ejecting, and cocking.

What size round does the M240 fire?

7.62mm.

Name the different types of ammunition rounds for the M240.

Ball, tracer, armor piercing, blank, and dummy.

What is the standard distance for bore sighting the M240?

10 meters.

How long of a burst should an M240 gunner fire?

6-9 rounds.

Name the eight major components of the M240.

Barrel assembly, buttstock assembly, driving spring rod assembly, bolt and operating rod assembly, trigger housing assembly, cover assembly, feed tray, and receiver assembly.

What are the three methods used to reduce thermal stress on a weapon (overheating)?

Radiation, conduction, and convection.

How are threats prioritized when using the M240?

Most dangerous, dangerous, and least dangerous.

When multiple targets of the same threat level are encountered, how are targets placed in order of priority?

Near before far, frontal before flank, and stationary before moving.

How is recoil managed with the M240?

Recoil management is the result of the Soldier assuming and maintaining a stable firing position which mitigates the disturbance of the sight picture during firing.

A small change in aiming when firing the M240 can result in how much deviation at 300 meters?

Up to 18 inches.

What is the maximum range of the M240B?

3725 meters.

What is the weight of the M240B with barrel and with tripod?

27.6 lbs. with barrel, another 20lbs with tripod.

What is the maximum effective range of the M240B for a bipod/point target?

600 meters.

What is the maximum effective range of the M240B for a tripod/point target?

800 meters.

What is the maximum effective range of the M240B for a bipod/area target?

800 meters.

What is the maximum effective range of the M240B for a tripod/area target?

1100 meters.

What is the maximum effective range of the M240B for suppression of a target?

1,800 meters.

What is the maximum effective range of the M240B for grazing fire?

600 meters.

What is the tracer burnout for the M240B?

900 meters.

What is the sustained rate of fire for the M240B?

100 rpm, 6-9 rounds, 4-5 seconds, every 10 minutes.

What is the rapid rate of fire for the M240B?

200 rpm, 10-13 rounds, 2-3 seconds, 2 minutes.

What is the cyclic rate of fire for the M240B?

650-950 rpm, continuous burst/min.

M249 SAW

TC 3-21.76, FM 3-22.68

What FM covers the M249?

FM 3-22.68.

What is the maximum range of the M249?

3600 meters.

What is the maximum effective range for the M249 on a tripod area target?

1000 meters.

Describe the M249.

5.56mm gas operated, magazine or belt feed, automatic squad automatic weapon.

What is the weight of a M249 with barrel and with tripod?

16.41 lbs. with barrel, another 16 lbs. with the tripod.

What is the maximum effective range for the M249 on a bipod for a point target?

600 meters.

What is the maximum effective range for the M249 on a bipod on an area target?

800 meters.

What is the maximum effective range for the M249 for grazing fire?

600 meters.

What is the tracer burnout for the M249?

900 meters.

What is the sustained rate of fire for the M249?

50 rpm, 6-9 rounds, 4-5 seconds, every 10 minutes.

What is the rapid rate of fire for the M249?

100 rpm, 6-9 rounds, 2-3 seconds, 2 minutes.

What is the cyclic rate of fire for the M249?

850 rpm continuous burst/min.

Pistol

....

TC 3-21.75, TC 3-23.35

What is the maximum effective range of the 9mm pistol?

50 meters.

What manual covers Military Pistols?

TC 3-23.35.

Name the firing cycle in order.

Feeding, chambering, locking, firing, unlocking, extracting, ejecting, cocking.

What are the two types of grips when firing the service side arm?

01 and 2 hand grip.

Name the Major Components of the Military Pistol.

Slide assembly, barrel assembly, receiver assembly.

How do you know when you have a proper sight picture with the service pistol?

The dots on the rear and front sight posts are aligned in a straight line.

What is the muzzle velocity of the 9mm pistol?

1230 feet per second.

What is the maximum range of the 9mm pistol?

1800 meters.

Javelin

....

TC 3-21.75

Describe the Javelin.

The Javelin is the first fire-and-forget, crew-served antitank missile. The Javelin's two major components are a reusable Command Launch Unit (CLU) and a missile sealed in a disposable launch tube assembly.

What is the caliber of the missile the Javelin fires?

126 mm.

What is the maximum effective range of the Javelin?

2,000 meters.

What is the maximum effective engagement range of the Javelin in Direct attack mode?

65 meters.

What is the maximum effective engagement range of the Javelin in Top attack mode?

150 meters.

ADRP 1-0 Army Profession

ADRP 1-0, TC 7-22.7

What does the acronym ADRP stand for?

Army Doctrine Reference Publication.

Define stewardship.

Our duty to care for the people, other resources and the profession entrusted to us by the American people.

What is the bedrock of the Army profession?

Trust.

How do Army professionals maintain the trust of the American people?

By living and upholding the Army ethic.

As an Army professional you must develop expert knowledge in what four fields?

Military-technical, moral-ethical, political-cultural, and leader human development.

Define competence.

Demonstrated ability to successfully perform duties with discipline and to standard.

Define esprit de corps.

Denotes the Army's common spirit, a collective ethos of camaraderie and cohesion within the team.

What makes you a professional NCO?

Consistent demonstration of competence, character, commitment.

What subject does ADRP 1-0 cover?

The Army Profession.

What ADRP covers The Army Profession?

ADRP 1-0.

What was the first corps of the Army to be recognized as professional in nature?

The commissioned officer corps.

What is the Army Ethic?

The Army Ethic is an evolving set of laws, values, and beliefs, deeply embedded within the core of the Army culture and practiced by all members of the Army Profession to motivate and guide the appropriate conduct of individual members bound together by a common moral purpose.

Define commitment.

The resolve to contribute to honorable service to the nation and accomplish the mission despite adversity, obstacles, and challenges.

According to ADRP 1-0, what is our first task?

Develop expert knowledge.

What is the Profession of Arms?

A community within the Army Profession composed of Soldiers of the Regular Army, Army National Guard, and Army Reserve.

What often sets the Army apart as an institution?

Observing Army customs and traditions.

Define Traditions.

A customary pattern of thought, action, and behavior held by an identifiable group of people.

What are the two components of the dual nature of the Army?

It is both a military department and a military profession.

ADP & ADRP 2-0 Intelligence

ADRP 2-0, ADP 2-0, ATP 2-01.3, TC 3-21.75, TC 3-27-76

What subject does ADP 2-0 cover?

Intelligence.

What are the six intelligence processes?

Plan and direct; collect; produce; disseminate; analyze; and assess.

What is IPB?

Intelligence Preparation of the Battlefield.

What drives the commander's intelligence process?

Commander's guidance.

What ADP covers Intelligence?

ADP 2-0.

What does ISR stand for?

Intelligence, Surveillance, and Reconnaissance.

What does ES2 mean?

Every Soldier a Sensor.

What does PIR stand for?

Priority Intelligence Requirements.

What does RFI stand for?

Request for Information.

What does COA stand for?

Courses of Action.

What does CCIR stand for?

Commander's Critical Information Requirements.

What does the key word SALUTE mean?

Size, Activity, Location, Unit, Time, and Equipment.

What is the SALUTE report used for?

It is a concise report designed to provide military intelligence information to the chain of command.

What manual covers IPB of the battlefield?

ATP 2-01.3

What does the acronym IPB stand for?

Intelligence Preparation of the Battlefield

ADRP & ADP 3-0 Operations

....

ADRP 3-0, ADP 3-0, TC 3-27.76

What subject does ADP 3-0 cover?

Operations.

What is the Army's basic warfighting doctrine?

ADP 3-0.

ADRP 1-03 Universal Task List

What does PMCS stand for?

Preventive Maintenance Checks and Services.

What is the Army Universal Task List (AUTL)?

A comprehensive, but not all-inclusive listing of Army tasks, missions, and operations.

What does MDMP stand for?

Military Decision-Making Process.

What is the subject of ADRP 1-03?

The Army Universal Task List.

What ADRP covers the Army Universal Task List?

ADRP 1-03.

What is a flank attack?

A form of offensive maneuver directed at the flank of an enemy.

What does BDAR stand for?

Battle Damage Assessment and Repair.

RATER QUICK

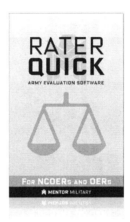

Now Designed for Both **NCOERs** and **OERs!**

**Fully up-to-date with the latest
Army Evaluations system!**

Contains:

- Hundreds of example bullets organized by Character, Presence, Intellect, Leads, Develops, and Achieves

- All the forms you need in one place

- Examples and advice from Senior NCOs and Officers

WEAR IT RIGHT!

Army Uniform Book & Uniform Tool

Solve all your uniform needs! Look your best for your next inspection or board, and do it FAST!

Wear it Right: Army Uniform Quick Reference Book: In this book you'll find the answers to all your dress and appearance questions. Uniform components are organized alphabetically so you can find what you need quickly and easily. Complete with uniform photo diagrams: Learn where everything is placed on your ASUs, Class Bs, and ACUs!

Army Uniform Tool: This best-selling tool makes looking your best easier than ever. With 6 calibrated templates you can ensure correct placement every time! **Scan the QR Code** for instant access to Uniform Diagrams, tool instructions and Army uniform regulations!

Get the *Wear it Right Book and Uniform Tool* at: MentorMilitary.com

The BOARD MASTER

Army Board Pocket Study Guide

21 Subjects Containing Over 650 Questions!

Master, 90% of the questions all U.S. Army Boards frequently ask. This helpful study guide **focuses on the most commonly asked** questions in Army Boards. Our research and experience demonstrates these questions are the most frequently asked and encompass 21 subject areas.

The Board Master:

- Is perfect for all board types: E-5/E-6, Soldier/NCO of the Quarter, Sergeant Morales or Audie Murphy
- Includes 2 example biographies and more helpful board information
- Flip card format makes studying quick and easy

Take The Board Master with you Anywhere.
Available in an App for IOS and Android. *Keyword: "Board Master"*

Get your copy of *The Board Master* at: MentorMilitary.com

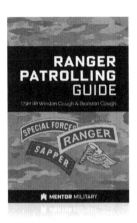

Ranger Patrolling Guide

Whether you are a Ranger, Looking to become a Ranger, or simply want to be knowledgeable on patrolling tactics, techniques, and procedures then this guide is for you. Learn from over 40 years of combined Infantry, Ranger, and Special Forces Experience.

When your position is ambushed, when crossing open danger areas, do you know exactly what to do? Don't think, know. Knowledge is the key to success and mission accomplishment. Arm yourself with the knowledge you need to succeed. A great how to tool for any leader regardless of MOS!

Get Ranger Patrolling Guide at: MentorMilitary.com

Land Nav: Basic to Advanced

In today's world, Soldiers rely heavily on their GPS. What are you going to do if you run out of batteries or the satellites go down? You better know how to use a map and compass. Land Navigation is a perishable skill. Possessing these skills will set you apart from the average Soldier.

The skills in this book range from basic to advanced. . The "Advanced" section covers field expedient methods, route planning as well as tips and tricks and a section on the Ranger School Land Nav course and the SFAS Land Nav course.

Get *Land Nav: Basic to Advanced* at: MentorMilitary.com

MENTOR MILITARY
FOR THE MILITARY PROFESSIONAL

Why Shop from **MentorMilitary.com?**

- Our product selection is curated specifically for servicemembers
- Competitive pricing, our prices are often beat Amazon
- Most orders ship within 1 business day
- We ship to APO/FPOs
- We offer a 30-Day Money Back Guarantee on our books

Books, Software, and Tools to Accelerate your Military Career